MORE
Energizers
and
Icebreakers
for All Ages and Stages

Book II

by

Elizabeth S. Foster-Harrison, Ed.D.

Copyright 1994
Educational Media Corporation®

ISBN 0-932796-64-8
Library of Congress Catalog No. 94-070342
Printing (Last Digit)

9   8   7   6   5   4

Publisher—

Educational Media Corporation®
PO Box 21311
Minneapolis, MN 55421-0311
(612) 781-0088

Production editor—
Don L. Sorenson

Graphic design—
Earl Sorenson

Illustrations—
Teresa LaBiche

Elizabeth S. Foster-Harrison

Dedication

To the person who has truly energized my life, to my friend and husband, Tony.

A special thank you to friends and colleagues who continue to provide the fertile ground on which energizers and icebreakers grow: Judy White, who gave the energizer's video a place to happen; Marcia McLendon, a supporter in all energizer endeavors; Bonnie Kane and the rest of the spring 1992 graduate class for being such great guinea pigs; Teresa LaBiche for her sparkling art work; Shannon Smith for getting all the words into a computer; JoLynn Johnson who always tells me how creative she thinks I am—so I almost believe it!

And a personal thanks to Caroline and Golda, who continue to inspire a belief in yet more to come.... Thank you.

About the Author

Elizabeth S. Foster-Harrison has enjoyed a career with many opportunities and varied roles. She has been a teacher, state and national consultant, peer helper coordinator, curriculum supervisor, childbirth educator, university professor, author, and poet.

She has contributed to the field of peer work as President of the North Carolina Peer Helper Association, President of the National Peer Helpers Association, as author of the highly successful student text *Tutoring: Learning by Helping,* and she continues to serve on the Board of Directors of the National Peer Helper Association as Immediate Past President.

Elizabeth Foster-Harrison completed her doctoral work at North Carolina State University where she focused her research on peer tutoring training models.

Elizabeth's highly acclaimed *Energizers and Icebreakers for all Ages and Stages,* her first energizers book, became a standard reference for teachers, counselors, and group leaders. The wide use of that book propelled Elizabeth to respond to requests for more!

Elizabeth makes her home in Greenville, North Carolina with her daughter, Tiffany; son, Christopher, and husband, Tony. She is currently employed in the School of Education at East Carolina University in Greenville.

About the Artist

Teresa LaBiche received her bachelor of fine arts degree in theatre design from the University of Southern Mississippi. She is currently pursuing a masters degree in elementary education at East Carolina University.

Ms. LaBiche enjoys working in a variety of mediums and uses her gift of visual expression to share the wonderment of life with others.

Table of Contents

Preface

This book is written to guide, assist, and stimulate the group leaders, counselors, peer professionals, peer helpers, and teachers who work with others and believe in active learning.

The process of learning is a complex and continuous one. It is often said that once we know what we don't know, we really begin to know. This concept is confirmed many times as people work with new groups, new classes, and new trainees. We learn from others as we watch them grow from participation in a learning environment which promotes interaction, involvement, and reflection. Learning is a process of growth that depends on interaction between the environment and people. Without involvement, a passive receptivity becomes the mainstay, an approach which has shown to be less effective, less long lasting, and certainly less enjoyable.

The use of energizers and icebreakers requires its participants to be directly involved. It requires an attitude of commitment to the task. The focus of each person and group supports the notion that stimulation will increase learning and participation.

The activities in this book are designed for all ages and stages and types of groups. The variety of strategies provide a multitude of methods developed to create a learning environment which is inviting, warm, stimulating, and challenging. While some activities may be done just for fun, others may be selected for specific skill development. Whatever your choice, it will be evident that the activities can be adapted to any age or number of people participating.

General guidelines are included in each section for management, icebreakers, and energizers. Following these suggestions will insure success when carrying out these activities. Read through each and follow for maximum results. A sure recipe for success!

Chapter I
Management

Judy McDuffy (L) and Trena Peacock (R) work with leader Elizabeth Foster-Harrison to organize sessions and get materials ready.

Elizabeth S. Foster-Harrison

Overview of Management

Interactive activities require a commitment to the growth of a group through a number of developmental exercises. These activities can be designed to help the group members get to know each other better so they are more effective in their tasks, or they can be designed to teach skills through movement and involvement.

The type of activities related to a group getting to know each other are generally called icebreakers. Some may call them "warm-ups," "getting to know your groups," "orientation sessions," or "boundary breakers." Regardless of the term, the purpose is to better prepare a group to work together.

Activities that are designed to specifically arouse the group or stimulate their creative responses are called "energizers." These activities generally involve movement, some amount of noise, and a great deal of interaction.

Both icebreakers and energizers support the learning models which embrace participant involvement and learning through action. While many people want to use these types of methods in their groups, classrooms, peer training groups, or staff development exercises, many people hesitate for one major fear. That fear is the fear of a lack of control. Because uncontrolled chaos is disruptive and unproductive, this chapter is included as a means of helping the novice "experiential" facilitator, as well as the seasoned facilitator, to structure the sessions to maximize success in learning and development.

The first section in this chapter deals with "Ways to Group" (1.1). It is important to use a variety of strategies to group your participants. Full group development in the form of trust and cohesion can only occur as the participants have an opportunity to work with all members, not just a select few. Special friends and other types of cliques can easily form without any notice; therefore a deliberate approach to mixing the groups encourages greater diversity, sensitivity, and understanding.

The second area, "Ways to Pair" (1.2), is based on the same premise as the grouping rationale. Both the pairing and grouping methods also provide creative ways to model for your participants how they can also structure groups or pairs. This is particularly helpful if you are working as a "trainer of trainers." The modeling of strategies can be easily replicated.

"Ways to Select Leaders" (1.3), the third section, is not designed to screen for leadership qualities. This area is designed for a mixing of leading and facilitating skills. The suggestions in this area are more related to diverse and random selections for small or full group leaders. If your activity requires a specific skill to lead, then you might select your leader based on that specific skill.

The fourth section, "Ways to Vote" (1.4), is designed to help the group facilitator vary the means by which consensus is reached. There are suggestions for voting by moving physically from one location to another, or more simply, holding a thumb up or down. But again, the purpose is to vary the way data is collected.

The section on "Pointers" (1.5) deals with concrete objects you can use to point with. At first glance the reader might think that the pointer section deals with hints for management, instead of concrete objects to use. It's fun to have a variety of objects that the leader and participants can use to emphasize visual information. It's more stimulating and certainly more colorful to see someone hold a star wand or cane to use to point to something, rather than always using an index finger.

The last area, "Ways to Line Up" (1.6), is a list of ways to organize the participants in rows or columns. This is a list that can be enlarged. Send your ideas to me on this area or any other area. I'd love to hear about ideas that have worked. You could see your idea (with credit, of course) in the next energizers book!

I have included some guidelines for facilitators of energizers and icebreakers. Be sure to follow them for a successful "getting to know you" period.

Guidelines

1. **Be patient.** Building trust and creating support don't happen overnight. This is a time consuming process. As a group facilitator you need to exercise patience and tolerance for people as they change and grow. It's always good to remember to keep a sense of humor about all of this so you manage to keep a set of standards that allows your patience to stay in check.

2. **Sequence the activities appropriately.** Be sure you select your sequence of activities in a way that is appropriate for your group. If the participants don't know each other at all, the sessions should be non-threatening in a non-revealing format until everyone is comfortable.

3. **Be prepared.** For the involvement and interaction to be smooth and organized, you must have all the materials you'll use at your fingertips. There is little else that makes a leader appear less able to lead than not having things organized and ready. Take the extra time to have everything ready. Be sure to read over the directions if you are trying an activity for the first time.

4. **Model attitudes!** Be sure that you are exemplary in your ability to demonstrate enthusiasm and interest in the activities. Be sure to participate whenever you can. In fact, one of the modeling techniques is to model the first response for the group so they understand the expectation. Smile and have fun!!

5. **Establish guidelines.** Outline for your participants what the framework will be during the energizer and icebreakers activities. You may wish to incorporate the wishes of your participants in the design of your guidelines. If this is your style (and I encourage this flexibility), be sure to have a set of guidelines in your head so that you can lead your group to include the items you need to have in place in order to be successful. Be sure to deal with areas such as movement, sound, listening, participation, and materials. Group members can have specific roles/assignments such as the (a) facilitator, (b) materials gatherer (c) recorder (d) reporter (e) checker. Whether you are working with young participants or adults it helps to have a system in place to assist you organize the movement and assignments. Everyone should understand the responsibilities of being a group member. If this is a new experience for the participants then you may have to actually practice some of the behaviors that have been outlined. This is great to do. It ensures greater success later.

6. **Provide time for reflection.** Be committed to always taking the time to provide opportunities for reflection, opportunities to review the purpose of the activity or the skill developed. It is important to remember that there are goals for learning beyond just feeling good. If the group doesn't have this chance than they will not know if they reached their goal and the leader will have the same difficulty .

Provide time to discuss with participants the purpose and outcome of the activity. Circles are good for maximizing contributions and participation.

Have a wonderful time using all of these activities. Stay well organized and managed and you'll find the process one that is stimulating for all participants and you, too!

Management 1.1
Ways to Group

Participating faculty members from D.H. Conley High School work in individual groups to accomplish an assigned task.

Number of people:

Unlimited

Time:

Dependent on each organizational activity

Materials:

Vary

Purpose:

To provide a structured way to group people

Description:

The different ways to group people listed below are simply creative ways in which people can be organized. Remember, the key to using energizers and icebreakers deals with the understanding of flexible organization, but specific guidelines ensure success.

1. People can be grouped by colored dots. Each dot represents a group.

2. The old standby of numbering off still works, all similar numbers become a group.

3. Animal sounds can be distributed and the participants must make the appropriate sound to find their group. A particular activity around animals can be found in *Energizers and Icebreakers—Book 1*, Energizer 2.32, p. 121.

4. Playing cards can be used to group people in fours by the type of suit—such as hearts, diamonds, spades and clovers. Numbers can also be used—odd, even, first third, second third, third third of numbers, and so forth.

5. Put names, words, or feelings on cards. These would be items that people could act out or express to find their group.

6. Pictures could be placed on cards that represent favorite foods, vacation sites, hobbies, books, and so forth. The same number would need to be duplicated for the number in the group.

7. Use puzzles that can be commercially purchased or handmade. The number of pieces would indicate the group size. Pieces would be randomly distributed and then members would find their group by matching their pieces.

8. Comic strip frames could be clipped out and then laminated. Separate the frames and randomly distribute them. This allows individual members to look for their group by comic strip and also get in a particular sequence.

9. Circus partners could be found by duplicating the different roles in the circus. There would be four clowns, four ringmasters, four acrobats, and four animal trainers. (This would represent a group of l6.) Other roles could be used. Pictures could be drawn also. People would act out their roles to find their common group.

10. If the grouping activity is near any holiday, give cards to the participants for that holiday to group them. Use four or five alike to create the groups. Different colors or shapes could be used to simplify the process.

11. Use famous people who belong to a certain career or organization. These names would be placed on cards, or if available, the name and picture. An example of categories: famous military people, famous singers, famous politicians, famous artists, famous writers, famous actors, famous dancers, famous designers, famous scientists, famous historical figures, famous cartoon figures, famous TV personalities, famous sports figures (and those could be separated by sport), famous educators, and so forth. The participants would then move through the group with their card and the noted person's name on it, asking others about the kind of profession they were in. They would continue until they found people in a similar career or were famous for similar activities.

12. Cut out newspaper articles. Divide the articles in three, four, or five parts. Distribute them and have participants find the other pieces of the article to make a whole. Give one member the headline.

13. Draw the silhouette or outline of different people or animals. Cut these apart so that it would resemble a puzzle. Distribute randomly the pieces and have people find their groups by locating the other parts to the people or animals.

Management 1.2
Ways to Pair

Number of People:

Unlimited

Time:

Dependent on the type of organizational strategy

Materials:

Varies

Purpose:

To provide creative and structured ways to pair participants for activities

Description:

There are many different ways to pair participants. It is always more fun to be creative and allow participants the exploring opportunity of finding a matched partner. By varying the ways we pair, we give participants a better chance of getting to know more people and interacting in a variety of ways.

A. Listed below are some animal sounds. Make two sets and cut the sounds apart. These should then be randomly distributed so members can find their partners by making the sounds and finding their like animal friend. This list of 15 animal sounds is for a group of 30 people. For a smaller group, just reduce the number of slips of paper that represent the sounds.

   1. Tweet tweet (bird)
   2. Neigh (horse)
   3. Quack quack (duck)
   4. Who-o-o-o (owl)
   5. Bzzzzzzzzz (bee)
   6. Hee Haw (donkey)
   7. Squeak Squeak (mouse)
   8. Moo moo (cow)
   9. Oink oink (pig)
   10. Growl (lion)
   11. Bark (dog)

Elizabeth S. Foster-Harrison

12. Rattle (snake)

13. Baaa Baaa (sheep)

14. Meow (cat)

15. Gobble gobble (turkey)

B. Have people match up in the pairs based on any of the following directions:

1. with the same shoe size

2. have similar patterns in their thumbprints

3. same favorite ice cream

4. same height

5. in the same profession, same length of time

6. same initials—either first or last name or a combination

7. same zodiac sign

8. alphabetically, match 1 with 2, 3 with 4, 5 with 6, 7 with 8, and so forth....

9. same age

10. same eye color/different eye color

11. same hair color/different hair color

12. same change or close to amount in pocket or purse

13. same hand size

14. same shoulder height

15. same number of siblings

16. same state or city of birth

17. same/different political party

18. people pair, flip two coins.... If the coins are the same, they stay together, if not, they go to the next person, until they flip a coin and match a partner.

19. can demonstrate the same dance step.... example, one person may be doing the polka and look for someone else doing the polka, one may be doing the Texas Two-Step and look for a partner doing the same thing.

20. favorite way to spend the summer

21. same number of traffic violations

22. same hair length

23. same favorite movie

24. same favorite sport—show the skill of some sport and find a partner doing the same thing.

C. Similar to the animal sounds, duplicate this list of songs and give each participant a slip of paper with the song titles. Participants move through the room humming or singing the song and looking for a partner humming the same song. This can also be done in a grouping exercise with more people in the group than two. This list of 16 would be for a group of 32. Reduce the number of songs for a smaller group.

1. Nick Knack Paddy Whack, Give a Dog a Bone

2. London Bridge is Falling Down

3. Three Blind Mice

4. Happy Birthday to You

5. I've Been Working On the Railroad

6. A Tisket, A Tasket, A Green and Yellow Basket

7. Twinkle, Twinkle Little Star

8. Ten Little Indians

9. Rock-a-by Baby, In the Treetop

10. Rudolph the Red-nosed Reindeer

11. Frosty the Snowman

12. I'm a Little Teapot

13. It's Raining, It's Pouring, the Old Man is Snoring

14. Mary Had a Little Lamb

15. Row, Row, Row Your Boat

16. Whistle While You Work

Elizabeth S. Foster-Harrison

Management 1.3
Ways to Select Group Leaders

Number of people:

One per group

Time:

No time designation—one minute

Materials:

None necessary

Purpose:

To provide a creative and varied way to identify group leaders. The purpose of varying the approach is to share the opportunity and responsibility. This method is a fun, random, and fair way to share the facilitative role.

Directions:

Place the participants in groups by whatever way the trainer/teacher chooses. Once the group is in place, they will then have to select their individual group leader based on the instruction of the trainer. Use any of the following ways, if in fact the role is not skill dependent. If everyone is capable of carrying out the function, then the following suggestions will work well. You may try varying the methods throughout the leader selection process. Members can also brainstorm ways to select leaders and add to this list.

Select the person to be leader in your group who

1. has a birthday closest to January 1.
2. has the smallest shoe size
3. is the tallest group member
4. has the greatest number of buttons
5. has the longest hair
6. has the brightest colors of clothes
7. has the most jewelry on
8. is closest in age to the average age of the group
9. is the youngest group member

10. is the middle in height of all the group members
11. has the largest hands
12. has the longest life line on the palm
13. has the darkest or lightest hair color
14. has a first name that begins with or is closest to M
15. has a last name that begins with or is closest to T
16. has the greatest number of letters in both the first and last names
17. has the boniest knees
18. has the shortest pinkie finger
19. has the greatest number of rings on
20. has the lightest eye color
21. has the longest fingernails
22. has the largest, oldest, or fanciest watch
23. ate the healthiest breakfast
24. watched the least amount of TV the day before
25. exercised the greatest amount the week before
26. was at a movie most recently
27. read the last book
28. has the oldest pet
29. has the most unusual pet
30. has never smoked

Management Strategy 1.4
Ways to Vote

Number of People:

Unlimited

Materials:

(You will only need one of these items for each vote.) Dots, markers, chart paper, 5 x 7 cards

Time:

Varies

Directions:

Listed below are different ways that you can solicit votes from the participants on issues, positions, topics, or decisions. It is a good idea to vary the strategies. Group members will find the variety more interesting.

1. Have the topics listed on the top of chart paper—one topic per chart. Post the charts on the wall. Have the people place a dot or mark or design to represent their vote on the chart paper. If it's important to know how people voted, they can sign their name or initials.

---

2. Use a thumbs up for a group vote for "yes" and a thumbs down for "no."

3. Use 5 x 7 cards around the room with the following: Strongly Agree, Agree, No Opinion, Disagree, and Strongly Disagree. Call out the topic or issue and have the people move to the part of the room which best represents their position.

4. Use 5 x 7 cards as described above, but use a number system with 5 as high and 1 as low.

5. Use a sound system with certain sounds representing a yes, no, maybe, and no position. Examples: animal sounds assigned to each of the positions, automotive or machine sounds, songs, nursery rhymes, certain notes.

6. To give the sensation of how a majority of votes on one side might feel intimidating to another position, give some sound instrument to only one side to demonstrate their vote. Example: All the pro positions would ring bells and the con positions would use a thumbs up sign. That could then be reversed. Other instruments: kazoos, flutes, jingle bells, tambourines, drums, and whistles.

7. Use cards prepared with a + or a — on them to represent positive or negative. The cards would be held up by either individuals—if the vote is an individual vote—or a group representative would provide the vote for the group on behalf of the group—if the group had to confer and reach consensus.

8. Use different colored handkerchiefs or bandanas for group voting. Each group has three handkerchiefs or bandanas. One red for no, one green or blue for yes, and white for no opinion.

Management 1.5
Using Pointers

Purpose:

To provide creative visual approaches to points of emphasis

Discussion:

Pointers that are used in group work can be fun and create a lively informal atmosphere. If you are using visual material in your presentations, trainings, or group work then the use of "fun" type pointers can definitely add zest to the visual experience.

Suggestions:

1. A laser pointer that is used across the room to emphasize something on a transparency or chart can be effective, because you can be a long distance from the object, still manage the back of a room and focus the group on specific information that they are seeing in the front. Just be careful of people's eyes.

   A suggested source:

   Damark Company
   7101 Winnetka Avenue North
   PO Box 29900
   Minneapolis, MN 55429-0900

   1-800-827-6767

   Price: Approximately $70.00

2. Star wands are fun to use as pointers. Because of their size, they generally are used as pointers with items such as flip charts or other types of wall charts. They can also be used to tap a person on the head to identify the next speaker or contributor.

3. The expandable "pen-like" pointer which telescopes to about 24 inches can be used on an overhead, to point to the transparency on the wall, or a wall chart. This is an inexpensive type of pointer and easily carried in a training kit, bag or purse. They cost about $6.00 and can be picked up at most office or school supply stores.

4. Using a regular pen or pencil on a transparency to point to a particular item is an easy way to select something that you would like to highlight. It can sit on the overhead while you are discussing the particular transparency. Other items that are fun to use are cardboard cutouts that have a shape of an animal, or a finger or hand. There are some great pencils that have animal tops to them and the top can make a fun silhouette on the transparency. Even a strong pointed paint brush can make a good pointer for a transparency.

5. A fun type of pointer for larger areas is a cane from the old hat and cane era. There are a variety of types of canes that can be purchased, but the black cane is a good standby, it's light in weight and fits in most suitcases.

6. A narrow wooden dowel can be used as a pointer. Several different types of tops can be glued or drilled into the top to make unusual pointers.

7. Going to a craft shop can yield many different items to be used for a pointer on a transparency. There are straws, popsicle sticks, and even fancy clock hands which look interesting on the machine. A good craft shop is a leader's good friend. So scavenge through one that is close to you and see how creative you can be. Let me know some of the things you make or create!

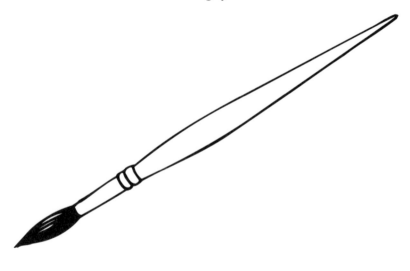

Elizabeth S. Foster-Harrison

Management 1.6
Ways to Line Up

Number of People:

Unlimited

Time:

5 to 10 minutes

Materials:

None necessary

Purpose:

To provide a variety of ways to organize the participants in rows or columns

Directions:

Have the participants organize themselves through the use of any of the following. They can line up through "soundless" experiences—nonverbally—or verbally. The choice is yours.

1. Alphabetically—first name first—then reorganized through last name.
2. Shoe size—small to large, large to small.
3. Ring size—large to small, small to large
4. Height—shortest to tallest, tallest to shortest
5. Age—youngest to oldest, oldest to youngest
6. Social Security number
7. Date of Birth—month
8. Hand size —large to small, small to large
9. Hair color—darkest to lightest
10. Driver's License—last four digits
11. By color of clothes: red 1st, blue, brown, green, and so forth

Elizabeth S. Foster-Harrison

Chapter II
Icebreakers

This icebreaker was done for a graduate class for members to get to know each other.

Elizabeth S. Foster-Harrison

Overview of Icebreakers

This chapter on icebreakers is an important one in the development of a group. This section provides activities which will assist the leader in creating an atmosphere within the group that is warm, inviting, and inclusive. The important stage of group growth at the onset of group work cannot be overemphasized. Utilizing the activities in this chapter to develop the different skills for group work will improve the approach and attitude of all participants, because it's fun and non-threatening to be involved.

Building trust and creating support is not something that happens quickly. As the group leader or facilitator you will need to exercise patience as you work with your participants. Pay attention to the requirements of the activity to assess whether your group is ready for a particular level of involvement. At the onset of group participation, it is recommended that the leader begin with low-risk types of interactions. Build toward activities which encourage more involvement, sharing, and participation.

The question many people ask is, "Why use icebreakers?" Another question is, "Who should use icebreakers?" The answer to both questions is quite simple. Everyone who serves in a group, and we all do at some point, really benefits from getting to know the people with whom we will engage in tasks and activities. It is more comfortable to know the people with whom we work, are in class, or have jobs in common.

To better enable a group to function comfortably and efficiently should be the primary consideration of all responsible leaders. Icebreakers that develop a feeling of cohesion on the part of the participants allows all members to work cooperatively toward accomplishing any assigned task.

A simple activity which begins with looking at our names is not quite so simple when it requires analyzing how we feel about ourselves and then sharing that information with others. This experience enables participants to not only look at their own individual meanings, but to see how others look at names or the characteristics associated with names.

Goals should be mutually established by the group so that everyone is working in the same direction. That way, when the group reaches its goal, the group will know it!

Icebreakers are fun! They are learning experiences that allow us to work together as people first and co-workers or learners second. We learn best when we are actively involved and feel comfortable in the group to which we are assigned. Therefore, using a variety of icebreakers will help develop the kind of atmosphere which leads to comfort, security and trust, which, in turn, creates willing learners and participants.

Icebreaker 2.1
Group Profile

Number of people:

Unlimited

Materials:

Charts with appropriate sketches, sticky dots

Time:

10 minutes

Skills:

Comparing similarities, analyzing graphic representations

Directions:

Place on the wall approximately six of the charts shown next. Instruct the participants to place a dot (one per chart) on the appropriate place on each chart to represent information about them.

Discussion:

Have the participants bring all the charts to the front of the group to analyze what characteristics the members had in common. The discussion should also provide time to look at the group as a whole, making generalizations about the group as a whole and individuals singularly.

Variation:

The artwork on the preceding page can also be used as a template to describe potential characteristics of those characters on the page. The characteristics can be written within each outline.

Elizabeth S. Foster-Harrison

Chart 1
Hours of Television Watching
Per Week

16
15
14
13
12
11
10
9
8
7
6
5
4
3
2
1

Chart 2
Where Were You Born?

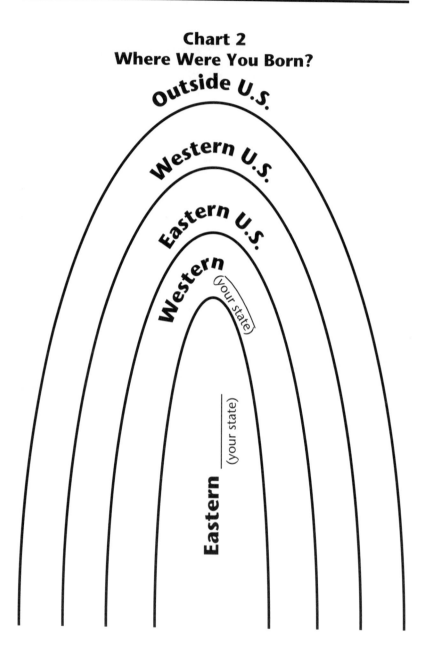

Outside U.S.

Western U.S.

Eastern U.S.

Western (your state)

Eastern (your state)

Elizabeth S. Foster-Harrison

Chart 3
Hours of Exercise
Per Week

0-1	2-4	3-5	6-8	9-10	11+

Chart 4
Eyes and Hair Chart

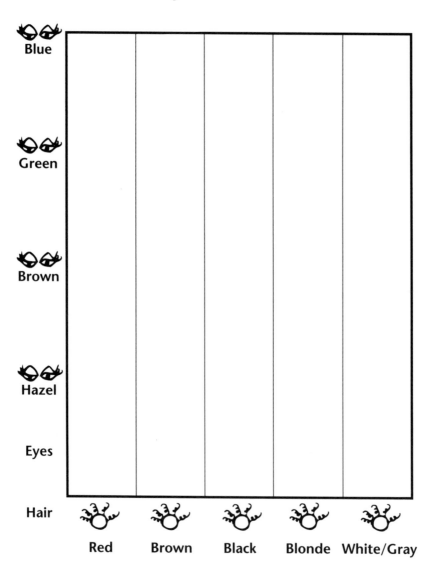

Elizabeth S. Foster-Harrison

Chart 5
Number of Siblings

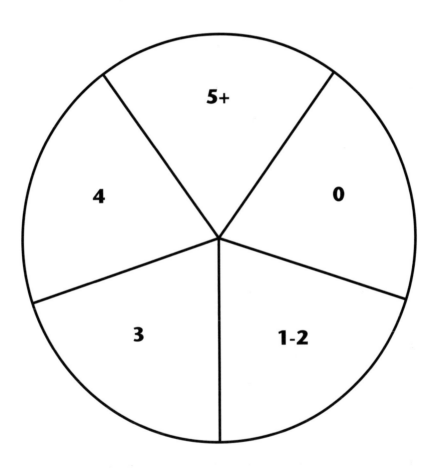

Chart 6
Pets

Dog	**Cat**
Fish	**Bird**
Rabbit	**Horse**

Other:

Chart 7
Favorite Types of Books

Chart 9
Favorite Ice Cream

Elizabeth S. Foster-Harrison

Icebreaker 2.2
Wearing the Name Tag

Number of People:

Unlimited

Materials:

Yarn, glitter, crayons, markers, cut out pictures, dots, lace, and 3 x 5 cards (and any items that could be used to decorate)

Time:

20 to 30 minutes

Directions:

A table should be set up with all the materials that could be used to decorate the 3 x 5 cards. The first name of each participant is written in big letters on each 3 x 5 card. Each participant can prepare the name tag as best represents the personality as each person sees it. Plan 10 to 15 minutes to prepare the tags.

Processing:

The participants can be placed in small groups to share their names and the significance of the decorations. If the group is small then the individuals can share with the full group. If the numbers are large, people can be paired and share with one other person. Remember this is an opportunity for the participants to get to know each other better, so encourage sharing and creativity.

The Group Hunt

Elizabeth S. Foster-Harrison

Icebreaker 2.3
The Group Hunt

Number of People:

Unlimited, Groups of 5 to 6 people

Material:

One piece of chart paper and marker per group

Time:

20 minutes

Skill:

Consensus building, understanding new people and groups

Directions:

Divide the participants into groups of 5 to 6 people each. Explain to the groups that they will be first *individually* filling out The Group Hunt Sheet of paper which indicates their individual likes and dislikes and some experiences. They will then compare those within the group. On chart paper they will indicate their agreement to a common like or dislike, which represents the group, and place that on the chart paper.

Processing:

The groups should discuss within each group and outside with the entire large body what items were similar, what they could agree on and what best represented that group. Points to make include how alike and different we all are, as well as how we may have similar experiences, and that we do not know whether others feel particularly happy or sad.

Variation: Cooperative Hunt

Renumber members within each group. Example: if there are five members in each group, then they each take a number 1-5. Use the "Cooperative Hunt" sheet within the group. Every person fills it out individually first. Then each member adds items from the group members. When completed, the groups re-order as in a "jigsaw" activity. All the number ones meet, the twos, the threes, and so forth. The new group shares the information from their "Cooperative Hunt Sheet" and each member adds more to the list. When completed they return to their original group to share all the new information.

The Group Hunt Sheet

Item	Like	Dislike
Food		
Movie		
TV Show		
Outdoor Game		
Holiday		
School Subject		
Chore at Home		
Hobby		
Book		
Video Game		

Elizabeth S. Foster-Harrison

Cooperative Hunt Sheet

Item	Describe the item or event
A time parents made you happy	
A time you may have gotten in trouble	
A time you may have felt left out	
A time you were mad	
A favorite place you have visited	
A time you felt proud	
A time someone suprised you	

My Double in the Crowd

Elizabeth S. Foster-Harrison

Icebreaker 2.4
My Double in the Crowd

Number of People:

Unlimited

Materials:

Double Chart, pen or pencil

Time:

10 to 15 minutes

Directions:

Provide a *Double Chart* for each participant. Ask the members to indicate the information that they would include for themselves under SELF. After they have done that, they should find others within the group sharing the same item. A name should be put in the blank, only one name per blank (a different name in each blank), provided there are sufficient people in the group.

Processing:

Allow the participants to pair up with some of the people with whom they had something in common to share their sheets. Allow about 30 seconds and then have the pairs change again with someone else they had something in common with. Note how many people had a name for each item and how much people in the group had in common with others.

Double Chart

Item	Self	Participant
Astrological Sign		
Favorite Ice Cream		
Favorite Musical Artist		
Hair Color		
Favorite Flower		
Eye Color		
Height		
Shoe Size		
Number of Siblings		
Pets		
Favorite Poem, Poet, or Book		

Elizabeth S. Foster-Harrison

Icebreaker 2.5
How Do You Feel Today?

Number of People:
Unlimited groups (Work in groups of no more than six)

Materials:
Picture cards or symbols

Time:
10 to 15 minutes

Purpose:
To give group members an opportunity to express how they feel today or share preferences through discussion with "symbol" starters

Directions:
Gather a variety of pictures to represent categories that are listed. The pictures can be glued on 5 x 7 notecards or placed on cardstock and glued to popsicle sticks. The sticks allow the participants to hold the picture or symbol in front of them and to talk about their choices while readily showing the sign.

Select a category for the day. The participants find a picture that represents how they feel about the category and show that picture.

This activity can serve as a barometer for the day or group time. The following categories will provide discussion starters.

Elizabeth S. Foster-Harrison

Categories

1 What you'd like to be doing right now....
2 Type of career you'd like to have...
3 Who you'd like to be....
4 Where you'd like to go...
5 How you feel today....
6 What's important to you....

Items

For *category 1*, find pictures that represent:

skiing	swimming	sleeping
jogging	walking	football
baseball	basketball	eating
biking	planting flowers	cooking
watching TV	seeing a movie	reading
using a computer	driving	playing at the beach

For *category 2*, find pictures that represent:
(this list is one of types of jobs/careers)

firefighter	police officer	military
medicine	clown	teacher
gardener	zoo keeper	journalist
politician	athlete	game warden
movie star	sanitation worker	airline pilot

Category 3 (this list is one of famous people; you can use either careers or famous names)

Mickey Mouse	Sylvester Stalone	Bugs Bunny
Eleanor Roosevelt	Roy Rogers	Scarlett O'Hara
Gandhi	President Clinton	Michael Bolton
Martin Luther King	Michael Jordan	Michelangelo
George Washington	Shirley Temple	Superman
Cat Woman	Mother Theresa	Gen. George Patton

For *category 4*, find pictures that represent:

Hawaii	Africa	Disney World
Alaska	Australia	Mountains
Paris	London	Mexico
California	Boston	Alamo
Washington, D.C.	St. Louis	Indianapolis

For *category 5*, find pictures that represent:

Happy	Sad	Angry
Frustrated	Curious	Loving
Quiet	Tired	Excited
Disgusted	Interested	Peaceful
Fearful	Impatient	Playful

For *category 6*, find pictures that represent:

flowers	money	cars
clothes	babies	family
health	friends	traveling
sports	learning	success

Note:

Be sure to select the type of pictures that are age appropriate for the group with which you are working.

Variations:

a. The participants can draw the picture or symbol which represents their choice in that category.

b. The participants can cut out the pictures themselves and glue them to the cards.

c. Take a subject of controversy and have the signs represent a position on the topic. The signs could say: Strongly Agree, Agree, No opinion, Disagree, Strongly Disagree. As comments are made about the topic, different group members hold up the signs. There would need to be duplicates of the different position signs.

Icebreaker 2.6
Three New Friends

Number of People:
Unlimited

Materials:
Sound instruments for the movements, such as a horn, whistle, tambourine, clacker

Time:
10 to 12 minutes

Purpose:
Can be used as a pairing activity

Directions:
1. Instruct the participants that they will hear the sound of a bell which signals it is time to find a partner who has a birthday close to theirs. It can be the same week or month—just close. The key is to get into pairs. Once they have found their partners, they first give each other a "high 5" or a "low 5," then they are to tell their partners what their favorite birthday memory is. It can be about a gift, a party, or just the special day. Now, make a sound with one of the instruments (the bell) and send the participants on their way to find their birthday partners. Give approximately 30 seconds for sharing once the people are in pairs.

2. Next, instruct the participants to find a *new* partner who has a shoe size close to theirs. Use one of the sounds (horn). When they find that partner they should share information about where their shoes have traveled, how they fit, and how old they are. Once they have shared, they should be instructed to turn back to back with their partners and give each other a back rub. This makes tired feet so much more relaxed! By moving up and down, they can create a backrub!

3. Ring the bell—this should be a reminder to find the "birthday partner" and give a "high or low 5." It isn't necessary to share information with the partners this time.

4. Blow the horn—everyone should find their shoe partners and give a backrub.

5. Tell the participants they should now look for someone who (pick an appropriate category) (a) has been in the same line of work for the same number of years, or (b) has been a peer helper for the same length of time, or (c) likes the same favorite subject. Use the whistle or another sound to send them on their way. When they find the new partner, instruct them to tell why they like their work, job, subject, and so forth. When the sharing is complete, tell them they will give their new partner a "new friend—hello handshake." Clasp hands—shake once regularly, shake hands at the tips of the fingers, shake hands holding one member's thumb, and then wave at each other with fingers.

6. Start the process again. Ring the bell, blow the horn, and blow the whistle. Each time the partners change and they perform the action.

Elizabeth S. Foster-Harrison

Additions:

Other types of pairings could be: favorite ice cream, favorite TV show, favorite color, favorite sport.

Other actions could include: a patty cake activity, handshake over the back, hop on each leg two times and turn around in a circle twice, touch at elbows twice and left elbows twice—right knees twice and left knees twice.

Things that could be discussed/shared: Why you like a certain dessert and where you last ate it. How you are like your favorite TV or movie character. The athletic skills you possess and the sports you've played, how your favorite color makes you feel and in what clothes do you generally wear that color?

Comment:

No more than three partners should be introduced in one session. Remember this activity is designed to "get to know" new people, so too many will defeat the purpose. The sounds can be used throughout a training or classroom year or group experience to pair people.

Icebreaker 2.7
Three New Groups

Number of People:

Unlimited

Materials:

Sound instruments, colored dots

Time:

10 minutes

Purpose:

To provide a way to set up groups

Directions:

Prior to beginning, all participants should receive a colored dot with a number and letter on it. There should be the same number of different colors as there will be groups. For example, if you have 20 people and you want four groups, then there will be four colors. If there are 30 people and you want 5 groups, there should be five colors. The numbers on each dot would also represent the number of groups. If you want four groups, number the colored dots 1 to 4 and repeat. Be sure to vary the numbers and colors. The same is true for the letters. Listed below are the dot configurations for four groups with four people per group. Also included are letters for four groups.

Red Dots	Yellow Dots	Green Dots	Blue Dots
1	2	3	4
a	b	c	d
4	1	2	3
d	a	b	c
3	4	1	2
c	d	a	b
2	3	4	1
b	c	d	a

Dots can be placed on wrists or the back of hands so they are readily seen. Each person should be instructed to learn the dot color, letter, and number assigned so that later it will be easy to move to the assigned groups.

Instruct the first set of groups to organize. Start with the color groups. Have all people with red dots go to one corner, the blue dots another corner, and so forth. When they get there, give a big high 5 in the center of the group circle. Use one of the sounds to signal movement (tambourine). Hereafter, the sound will signify the group membership.

Next, instruct the number groups to organize and use a different sound (bell). Call locations for group 1, 2, and so on. When they each arrive they should clap for each other—first on the right, next to the left, and repeat.

Finally, call the locations with a whistle for the letter groups. Have the a's in one corner, the b's in another corner, and so on. When the group arrives, they should form a circle and give each a backrub or back scratch and continually walk around in the circle like a train, scratching the back of the person in front of them.

Comment:

You can vary the sound and what the groups do whenever you like. This system is a quick and fun way to organize groups quickly.

Icebreaker 2.8
Keep Standing... If You're....

Number of People:

Unlimited

Material:

Lists

Length:

5 minutes

Purpose:

To get to know each other, focus on certain topics of interest of the participants

Directions:

Use any of the following lists to do the "Keep Standing If..." activity: Swell at Wellness, Sportscaster Indicator, Fitness Quotient, Humor Gauge, Diet/Nutrition Gauge.

Have all of the participants stand. Go through each item on one of the lists. Ask the participants to keep standing if (an example: they know the most famous Yankee homerun hitter—from Sportscaster Indicator). Those who don't should sit. Use only one list per activity.

Discussion:

The group can identify what the general topic or category is and can generate new statements. What items on the list were of interest to the group members? How do they get to know each other better through these activities?

Elizabeth S. Foster-Harrison

Icebreaker 2.9
Swell at Wellness

Keep standing if...

1. You engage in some leisure sport or activity.
2. You have had a massage. . .or would like to.
3. You haven't smoked in 24 hours.
4. You floss teeth regularly.
5. You use your seatbelt regularly.
6. You have exercised at least 3 hours in the past week.
7. You have helped someone within the last week.
8. You generally maintain the weight you'd like to have.
9. You haven't had caffeine in 24 hours.
10. You haven't eaten chocolate in 24 hours.
11. You know the sunshine vitamin.
12. You can make a funny sound with your body.
13. You know who's on first.
14. You have ever played a practical joke.
15. You can laugh at funny things.
16. You smile more than you frown.
17. You have a ticklish spot.
18. You don't need a lint brush for your belly button lint.

Icebreaker 2.10
A Sportscaster

Keep standing if...

1. You know the most famous Yankee homerun hitter.
2. You know the sport in which the pennant is won.
3. Know why the links has nothing to do with chains of metal.
4. Lacrosse uses what kind of equipment.
5. You know what NCAA represents.
6. You can name 1 team from the Big 10, Big 8, and ACC.
7. You know what college team Wilt Chamberlain played for.
8. You know Pistol Pete wasn't a gangster.
9. You know "the Refrigerator" wasn't in cold storage.
10. Joe Namath was famous for his aid of what?
11. Jim Palmer was famous for his ads of what?
12. The "Big O" stands for what?
13. Mohammed Ali's name before he changed it?
14. Stalone's famous boxing character?
15. You know who Olga Korbut is.
16. Jan Stevenson & _____ represent what sports and what kind of collaboration?
17. If this man's last name was his predator animal,... he'd be called Larry Cat.
18. The former Chicago Bears coach who was well-known.
19. "Little Chrissy" played what sport?

Icebreaker 2.11
Ready for the Comedy Club

Keep standing if...

1. You can make a funny sound with your body.
2. You know who's on first.
3. You have ever played a practical joke.
4. You can laugh at funny things easily.
5. You smile more than you frown.
6. You know the comedian associated with "Thanks for the memory."
7. You know who Gary Larson is.
8. You've ever seen the Keystone Cops.
9. You can remember a joke you've been told.
10. You like telling jokes.
11. You like hearing jokes.
12. You know who played the character Clem Kadiddlehopper.
13. You know why Charlie McCarthy couldn't really talk.
14. You can make a face that looks like an animal.
15. You have a ticklish spot.
16. You have an "innie" "belly button."
17. You don't need a lint brush for your belly button lint?
18. You have laughed at something in the last 24 hours.

Icebreaker 2.12
On a great Diet!

Keep standing if...

1. You know the major vitamin in orange juice.
2. You eat at least two green vegetables within three days.
3. You have some sort of fruit daily.
4. You haven't had caffeine in 24 hours.
5. You haven't eaten chocolate in 24 hours.
6. You read the nutrition labels on boxed packages.
7. You pay attention to the fat content in food.
8. You don't eat cereal loaded with sugar.
9. You avoid high cholesterol foods.
10. You prefer white meat to dark.
11. You eat chicken and fish in preference to red meat.
12. You eat a balanced diet daily.
13. You drink several glasses of water and/or juice a day.
14. Frozen yogurt has replaced ice cream for you.
15. You know the sunshine vitamin.
16. You don't add food to your salt.

Elizabeth S. Foster-Harrison

Icebreaker 2.13
Score High on a Fitness Quotient

Keep standing if...

1. Can touch your toes without bending your knees.
2. Can do 20 sit-ups.
3. Walk, run, or jog three times a week.
4. Stretch before exercise.
5. Engage in some leisure sport or activity.
6. Use relaxation techniques.
7. Have had a massage,... or would like to.
8. Belong to a health club or have fitness equipment at home.
9. Take time for yourself—just for fun.
10. Have a plan for your health and wellness.
11. Haven't smoked in 24 hours.
12. Chew sugarless gum, if you chew.
13. Can balance on one foot for one minute with eyes closed.
14. Sleep at least six hours a night.
15. Think good personal hygiene is an important character quality.
16. Floss teeth regularly.
17. Use your seatbelt regularly.
18. Have exercised at least three hours in the past week.
19. Said something nice to someone in the last two days.
20. Have read a book for pleasure within the last three months.
21. If you helped someone with something in the last week.
22. You generally maintain the weight you'd like to have.

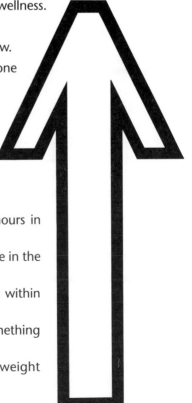

Icebreaker 2.14
More Scavenger Hunt Quests

Number of People:
Unlimited

Materials:
List of items to look for

Time:
10 to 15 minutes

Directions:
1. Hand out the Scavenger Hunt Sheet so each participant has a copy and explain the rules.

2. Each person has 10 minutes to obtain the greatest number of signatures from the members in the group. You can decide if there is a limit to the number of times any one individual can sign a sheet.

3. At the end of the 10 minutes, ask the participants to stop and add the total number of signatures.

4. VARIATION: If the entire group is large, divide the group into subgroups of four. The subgroups can move together and obtain signatures from other subgroups *or* members of the sub-group go out on their own to fill out their sheets. They then return to the subgroup to add their signatures. Determine which sub-group obtained the greatest number of signatures.

5. You can select from any of the following to create your own Scavenger Hunt Sheet:

Elizabeth S. Foster-Harrison

Quest

Names

1. Find three people who
   love chocolate.

   _____

   _____

   _____

2. Find one person who
   is a bird watcher.

   _____

3. Find two people who
   like to sing in the shower.

   _____

   _____

4. Find three people who
   have been reared in this state.

   _____

   _____

   _____

5. Find one person who
   has played on a tennis team.

   _____

6. Find two people who
   speak a foreign language.

   _____

   _____

7. Find one person who has the
   same favorite movie you do.

   _____

8. Find one person who has lived
   in the same house since birth.

   _____

9. Find three people with the same
   color hair as yourself.

   _____

   _____

   _____

10. Find two people with the same
    shoe size as yourself.

    _____

    _____

11. Find one person whose birthday
    is within 30 days of your own.

    _____

12. Find a person who has the
    same first initial as yours.

    _____

13. Find two people who
    look entirely different.

    _____

Quest

Names

14. Find three people who voted in
    the last presidential election.

    _____

    _____

    _____

15. Find two people who
    love chocolate ice cream.

    _____

    _____

16. Find one person who is the
    same height as yourself.

    _____

17. Find two people who talk
    on the phone 30 minutes a day.

    _____

    _____

18. Find three people who
    are tea drinkers.

    _____

    _____

    _____

19. Find two people who
    like snakes.

    _____

    _____

20. Find one person who
    has flown over 2,000 miles.

    _____

21. Find two people with
    the same astronomical sign.

    _____

    _____

22. Find one person who
    likes the same flower as you.

    _____

23. Find one person who had
    the same favorite season as you.

    _____

Icebreaker 2.15
Getting to Know Your Pumpkin

Number of people:

Unlimited.

Materials:

5 X 8 index cards, pens or pencils

Time:

15 minutes

Directions:

1. Pass out 5 x 8 index cards and ask the participants to place them on the table before them horizontally. Read the following instructions and pause after each item to allow time to complete the task. Read each item three times to clear up any misconceptions.

2. Leaving a one inch margin at the top of your card, draw as big an oval as possible, without touching any of the sides.

3. Divide the oval in half with a vertical line.

4. In the upper left hand quadrant of the oval, draw a triangle. Make sure the triangle is one inch high.

5. Divide the oval in half again by drawing a horizontal line.

6. About an inch to the right of the center of the top of the oval, draw a capital "C." Make sure to come as close to the top of the card and to the top of the oval, as possible.

7. Write the name you like to be called in the curve of the "C."

8. In the triangle, write your favorite color.

9. About one inch to the left of the center of the top of the oval, draw another "C" exactly as the first, except draw it backwards.

10. Draw another triangle about an inch high in the upper right hand quadrant of the oval. Write your favorite number in this triangle.

11. If you could be any animal in the world, what would it be? Write it in the curve of the backwards "C."

12. If you could have any three wishes in the world, what would they be? Place the answer in the lower left hand quadrant of the oval.

13. What one thing do you own that you would keep if you could keep only one thing following a disaster? Place that item in a triangle drawn in the center of the oval.

14. Make a list of your three most positive assets. Place that list in the lower right hand quadrant of the oval.

15. What one thing would you change about yourself if you could? Write it on the left side of the line that cuts the oval horizontally.

16. On the right side of the same line, write what job you would like to have if you could hold any job in the world.

17. What makes you angry? Write this between the two "C's" at the top of the card.

18. Think of one thing that makes you happy. Write this inside a banana, placed on its side drawn underneath the triangle in the center.

19. Connect the arcs of the top of the "C's" at the top of the card with a straight line . Happy Halloween !

20. Having completed the above questions, assign group members to pairs or small groups to share information. This activity can also lead to endless writing activities.

Adapted from Icebreaker 1.6, "Getting to Know Your Smile," in *Energizers, Book 1* by Kelly Roth, a student at East Carolina University.

Icebreaker 2.16
Self-O

Number of People:

10 to 20

Materials:

Self-O Cards and chips or beans to use as markers

Time:

20 to 30 minutes

Directions:

Using the blank SELF-O card, prepare as many cards as there are people in the group. The list below can be used to create the topics for the blocks. An example of a completed SELF-O card is included. Play like Bingo with a caller. The first person to have a diagonal, horizontal, or vertical line wins and has to call all the things that were covered on the winning Self-O card.

Likes to travel

Black hair

Enjoys school

Over 5 feet

Likes TV

Plays sports

Likes people

Blonde hair

Has a pet

Wears tennis shoes

Wears blue jeans

Under 5 feet

Brown hair

Likes to read

Blue eyes

Likes movies

Plays an instrument

Brown eyes

Has a bike

Clothes

Pizza

Ice cream

Long hair

Likes brunettes

Likes to go on picnics

Rides a bicycle regularly

Never eats onions

Always keeps a breath mint handy

Wears gloves when it is cold

Has at least two pets

Never gets bored

Is a real dancer

Has a Madonna tape or CD

Has seen *Pretty Woman* more than once

Would like to meet Kevin Costner or Cher

Has watched a fitness video

Would like smaller feet

Likes current weight

Self-O

S	E	L	F	☀
1				
2				
3		☀		
4				
5				

Elizabeth S. Foster-Harrison

Self-O

S	E	L	F	☼
1 Likes to travel	Black hair	Enjoys school	Over 5 feet tall	Likes TV
2 Plays sports	Likes people	Blonde hair	Has a pet	Wears tennis shorts
3 Wears blue jeans	Under 5 feet tall	☼	Brown hair	Likes to read
4 Blue eyes	Likes animals	Likes movies	Plays an instrument	Brown eyes
5 Has a bike	Likes clothes	Likes pizza	Likes ice cream	Has long hair

Icebreaker 2.17
GROUP-O

Number of people:

10 to 50

Materials:

A chart for each group, Velcro markers

Time:

20 to 30 minutes

Directions:

This is played similarly to Self-O (2.16), except that people play it in groups. There is one Group-O card per group. When any characteristic is true of one of the group members, then that person places a square on the square. There would be a Velcro piece on the back of the slips and in each block of the Group-O card so they can stick together. The winning group is the first one to get markers on a vertical, horizontal, or diagonal line.

Variation No. 1:

A variation of this would be to do a large chart with the GROUP-O blocks. It would be blank. There would be a place for two Velcro strips. As the caller calls the topic, the topic is placed on the first Velcro strip in the block. If a member of a team has that block, then he or she must first get to the block and put the square up. Again there would be a Velcro strip there for that. To distinguish among the groups, assign a different color marker for each group.

Variation No. 2:

Another variation would be to have items that have to be acted out by the group members or completed in front of the group. A suggested list is included.

Additional items for regular Group-O:

only drinks milk at dinner
thinks everyone should vote
would like to be in politics
keeps a checkbook
always keeps gas in the car
talks on the phone everyday
talks on the phone two hours a day

Elizabeth S. Foster-Harrison

is a well organized person
is very creative
likes to write
would like to be Mickey Mouse
believes in fairy tales
likes suspense movies
has seen two both Batman movies
is a tea drinker
plays a sport regularly

Variation 2 List

could have a cartoon voice
knows how to type
can sing
can do aerobic exercises
can dance
can touch toes without bending knees
can pout
can imitate a famous person
can look happy
can hiccup on command
would like to be a pilot
has an outie belly button
wishes to be a mountain climber
has a second toe longer than big toe
can give good back rubs
can sit cross legged on floor
has interesting dreams
can tell good jokes
has a funny laugh
can really snore
uses fingernails to tickle
can touch nose with eyes closed
can spell name backwards
can jump backwards 10 times
can pat head and rub stomach simultaneously
can make church and steeple out of hands

Variation on a Group

G	R	O	U	P
1				
2				
3				
4				
5				

Elizabeth S. Foster-Harrison

Variation on a Group

	G	R	O	U	P
1	Morning person	Thinks democracy should be taught	Has volunteered to help someone	Enjoys comedy movies	Practical joker
2	Like to dance	Likes to be in an airplane	Eats fruit	Gets 6-8 hours of sleep daily	Afternoon person
3	Finds math exciting	Would prefer a formal party to a picnic		A fish eater	Drinks at least two glasses of water a day
4	Enjoys Disney movies	Eats vegetables	Night person	Thinks it is OK for girls to call boys	Would like to fly to the moon
5	Talks on telephone	Night owl	Likes mysteries	Is a planner	Can sing

Icebreaker 2.18
The Interview Matrix

Number of People:

Unlimited pairs

Materials:

Interview Questions, Interview Matrix, pen or pencil

Purpose:

To get to know things about a partner

Directions:

Use the following questions to interview your partner. When you finish, fill out the matrix on your partner. Then check with your partner to see how close you are. The leader should then put pairs together and have each talk about their partners with the matrix.

Interview Questions

1. If you could buy any color shirt, what would it be? _____

_____

2. You enjoy what holiday the best? _____

_____

3. The majority of your leisure time is spent how? _____

_____

4. On a desert island, you'd pick this tape to play. _____

_____

5. With only one video to watch, what would it be? _____

_____

6. You'd spend $100.00 right now on what? _____

_____

7. Things you want to add to your wardrobe. _____

_____

8. Friends are important because.... _____

_____

9. An animal you'd prefer to be is a _____? Why? _____

_____

10. What famous person, living or dead, would you like to be? ____

_____

Interview Matrix for _____

1. What's important to your interviewee?

2. What is this person likely to do on a Saturday?

3. In terms of music, TV, or movies, what taste does your partner have?

4. What kind of person does your partner admire?

5. Ways your partner might spend money.

6. What makes a holiday fun for your partner?

7. What would a new outfit look like?

8. Buying a new pet might include:

Icebreaker 2.19
The Feeling Bag

Number of People:

Unlimited

Materials:

Bag—lunch bag size

Purpose:

To examine how holding feelings in can affect our behaviors and attitudes

Skills:

Identifying feelings

Directions:

1. The participants list on strips of paper different feelings that they could experience—one feeling per strip.

2. All the strips are put inside a bag. Each individual has a bag.

3. The discussion at this point involves speculation on what happens to people if they have no outlet for their feelings or if they keep everything bottled inside .

4. Everyone is then instructed to put the bag opening to their mouths and blow up the bag—tightly hold the top with one hand and then pop the bag. (This simulates what happens to feelings when there is no outlet.)

Discussion:

The participants then compare their speculation to the simulation. Behaviors associated with "Blowing up or apart" would be analyzed and then alternatives to "blowing up" could be discussed.

Elizabeth S. Foster-Harrison

Icebreaker 2.20
Crackerjacks

Number of People:

Unlimited

Materials:

Large Crackerjack box and strips of paper

Time:

10 minutes

Purpose:

To identify special gifts of everyone

Skills:

Perseverance

Directions:

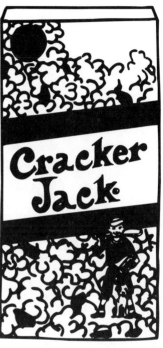

1. One large crackerjacks box should be placed on a table for the group. All the members write a positive characteristic on a strip which describes their best feature. Those are then folded and placed in the crackerjack box.

2. A discussion ensues which involves talking about where we find the prize in a crackerjack box—sometimes on the top, in the middle, or on the side, or on the bottom. How does the crackerjack box analogy apply to human characteristics? Do we always find someone's best characters at the beginning? In the middle? Pull out different strips and read aloud. Save some so that one can be read each day. More can be added. The group should clap to assure each participant's positive feeling.

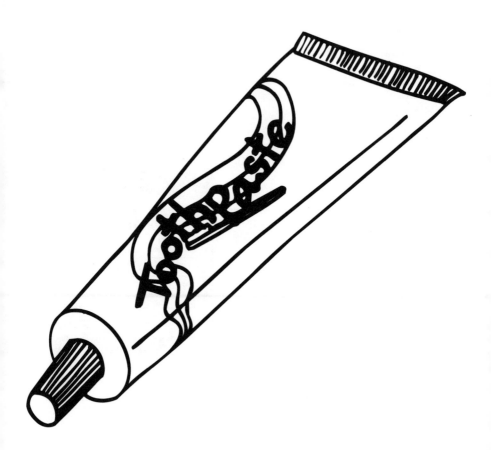

Elizabeth S. Foster-Harrison

Icebreaker 2.21
Toothpaste Confidence

Number of People:

Unlimited

Materials:

Toothpaste and box of tissue

Time:

5 minutes

Purpose:

This is a concrete demonstration designed to show the importance of confidentiality and to stress the critical nature of never breaking a confidence.

Skills:

Trust, integrity

Preparation:

Cover a box of toothpaste with construction paper so it fits tightly and place these words on the sides of the covered box: Trust, Confidentiality.

Cover tightly the tube of toothpaste with construction paper, writing on each side: Trust, Confidentiality. Be sure to leave the top open so it can be unscrewed.

Directions:

Show the box of toothpaste and ask the participants to define the words on the box. Take out the toothpaste. (Have your tissue handy.) Tell everyone that the toothpaste inside represents all the confidentiality built into helping relationships. As you continue talking, press some of the toothpaste out of the tube. "Oops—some has slipped out—someone shared information they shouldn't. Well, let's just put it back." Try putting the squeezed out toothpaste back in the tube. Of course it won't go back in. Wipe with tissue and make the point— once a confidence has been broken, it can not be put back together easily; much like Humpty Dumpty. As a reminder, tell everyone to think about confidentiality the next three times they squeeze their toothpaste to brush their teeth.

Icebreakers 2.22
Paper Dolls

Number of People:

Unlimited

Materials:

Scissors and pattern

Time:

20 to 30 minutes

Purpose:

Develop awareness of issues; perspectives on issues

Directions:

Give everyone a pattern and scissors. Then place on each figure, items from any of the following categories. Discussion occurs as the dolls are opened and people share what they placed on the paper cut outs. They can be posted to illustrate the variety of issues on the topic.

1. Problems young people face today.
2. Why we need helpers/volunteers in our society.
3. What make us happy?
4. What dreams do we have?
5. What are characteristics of leaders?
6. What motivates people towards success?
7. What are the greatest problems our schools face today?
8. How can communities collaborate to strengthen the safety of their citizens?
9. What gives people great satisfaction?

Elizabeth S. Foster-Harrison

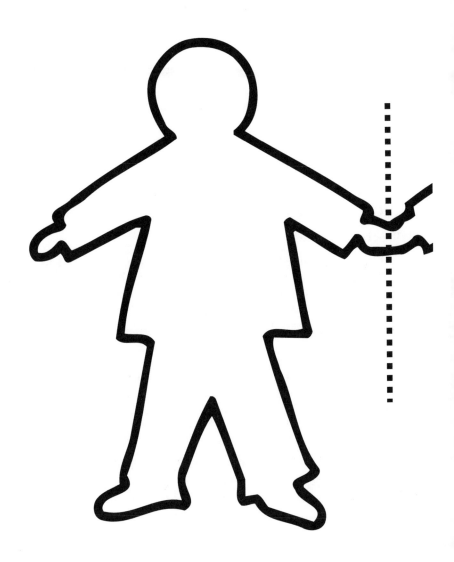

Paper Doll Pattern

Icebreaker 2.23
Treasure Hunt

Number of People:

10 to 20

Material:

Scavenger List, miscellaneous items, a paper bag for each participant

Time:

20 to 30 minutes

Purpose:

Get to know each other through discussion on the treasure hunt

Directions:

1. Instruct the participants to find specific items from others in the groups. They should have a sheet of paper which lists the items and then a space after each to describe why that is significant and the person's name from whom they got it. The participants need to be sure to write the person's name so each item can be returned.

2. Time the activity and call everyone together after 10 to 15 minutes. The activity can stop earlier if someone gets all of their scavenger hunt items. As the person who got the most items or all the items on the list begins to return them, a discussion can be held with the other participants showing the items they secured which represent the same areas.

3. This discussion can serve to help the group learn about each other and discuss what is important to them.

4. You can use items from wallets, purses, booksacks, self, or other locations.

Scavenger List

Find one item to represent the following. It might be helpful to have a bag.

1. Something sentimental
2. Something special that probably no one else has
3. Something worn on the feet
4. Something that makes a sound
5. Piece of jewelry
6. Something metal
7. Something that represents happiness
8. Something blue
9. Something hard
10. Something that represents another person
11. Something you can read
12. Something that's shiny
13. Something pointed
14. Something that smells good
15. Something 5 years old or older
16. Something soft
17. Something that can tear
18. Something with numbers
19. Something pretty
20. Something transparent.
21. A photo of someone
22. A coin
23. A metal object
24. Something soft
25. Something slick
26. An item of clothing
27. An item of jewelry

28. Something that holds clothess up or together
29. Something to do with hair
30. Something special to someone

Alternatives:

- Something made of leather
- Something you can smear, sniff, or put on
- Something for illness
- Something that holds something up
- Something that represents love
- Something someone gave you
- Something black

Icebreaker 2.24
Quotes To Use

Number of People:

Unlimited

Materials:

Quotes on a bulletin board, on butcher paper, flip charts, or construction paper

Time:

Not dependent on time, but integrated into other lessons or activities

Skills:

Integration of concepts through the use of quotes

Directions:

Listed below are a variety of favorite quotes that I have used over the years. They can be used for motivation, introducing a lesson, concluding a lesson or unit, developing a cohesive thought for a group or for group discussion. They may be used individually, or posted in a room for groups to discuss. They can be placed on individual transparencies to be used in visual presentations. The way you use them is dependent on your needs. Feel free to experiment. Have groups coin their own quotes to be added to the list. Some quotes may appear to be gender specific, but I believe those examples to be a product of the time. You may wish to make adaptations or modifications. Please acknowledge the source of the quote whenever you use one.

"Every minute in planning saves three or four in execution."

Crawford Greenewalt

"No one can make you feel inferior without your consent."

Eleanor Roosevelt

"In oneself lies the whole world and if you know how to look and learn then the door is there and the key is in your hand. Nobody on earth can give you either key or the door to open except yourself."

Iddu Krishnamurts

"It's hard to get directions if you don't know where you are."

Michael Mahoney

"The job of a friend is not to decide what should be done, not to run interference or pick up the slack. The job of a friend is to understand, and to supply energy and hope and in doing so to keep those they value on their feel a little longer, so that they can fight one more round and grow stronger in themselves."

Merle Shain

"Young people are not just the leaders of tomorrow —they have great untapped potential for responsible leadership TODAY!"

Brendtro, Brokenleg, Beckern.

"I don't care what you know, until I know that you care."

(original source unknown)

"We don't stop playing because we get too old, we get old because we stop playing.

(original source unknown)

"Young people cannot develop a sense of their own value unless they have the opportunity to be of value to others!"

Brendtro, Brokenleg, Becken.

"It is one of the most beautiful compensations of this life that no man can sincerely help another without helping himself."

Shakespeare

"One thing I know; the only ones among you who will be really happy are those who will have sought and found how to serve."

Albert Schweitzer

"I exist not to be loved and admired, but to love and to act."

Janusz Korczak

"Dreams are goals with wings."

Robert J. Kriegal

"Whatever one man is capable of conceiving, other men will be able to achieve."

Jules Verne

"Destiny is not a matter of chance, it is a matter of choice; it is not a thing to be waited for, it is a thing to be achieved."

W.J. Bryan

"The price of greatness is responsibility."

Winston Churchill

"Leadership is the art of getting someone else to do something you want done because he wants it done."

Dwight D. Eisenhower.

"Failure is only the opportunity to begin again more intelligently."

Henry Ford

"Injustice anywhere is a threat to justice everywhere."

Martin Luther King

"It's not whether you get knocked down, it's whether you get up."

Vince Lombardi

"You cannot shake hands with a clenched fist."

Golda Meir

"Give a man a fish and he can eat for a day. Teach a man to fish and he will eat for a lifetime."

Chinese Proverb

Elizabeth S. Foster-Harrison

"Deny a mistake, and you deny yourself the chance to learn from it."

Robert J. Kriegel

"A ship in port is safe, but that's not what ships are built for."

Grace Hopper

"There's as much risk in doing nothing as in doing something."

Trammell Crow

"I'd rather know some of the questions than all of the answers."

James Thurber

"Minds are like parachutes. They only work when open!"

Author Unknown

"Success in NOT a destination, It's a Journey!"

Mark Twain

"If there is not enough time to do it right, when will you find time to do it again?"

Malcolm F. MacNeil

Helping Tree

Icebreaker 2.25
The Helping Tree

Number of people:

10 to 50

Materials:

Post-It notes, pen or pencil

Time:

30 to 45 minutes

Directions:

1. Post on the wall a poster of a tree or a poster of the outline silhouette of a body shaped like a gingerbread man or have a person stand with back against wall standing with legs and arms out from the body. You can enlarge the artwork on page 94.

2. Members of the group are given approximately 5 small post-it notes.

3. The participants should think of characteristics of people who have been helpers to them during their lives. These could be friends, family, colleagues, students, mentors, teachers, anyone.

4. Once the post-its have been completed with one characteristic per post-it, each person goes up and places one post-it on the outline of the tree or silhouette—not repeating any already placed. Each person can call out the characteristic and define it as they interpret it.

5. This continues until all the characteristics have been placed.

VARIATION:

1. If the group is large, divide into sub-groups of 4 or 5. Have the subgroups create the characteristics on the post-its. Then members of the groups post the characteristics, one at a time.

2. Each subgroup could create their own "tree" or silhouette, but there would need to be a poster for each subgroup to do that.

PROCESS:

The discussion should include: the similarity of the "family tree" concept to a helping tree.... how a family creates roots, what roots mean towards creating stability, how a helping tree supports the whole group.... how all the characteristics represent helping.... how we should strive towards developing these attitudes, skills and characteristics.

Icebreaker 2.26
Taking a Stand

Number of People:

Unlimited

Time:

2 minutes for each issue

Materials:

5 X 7 cards to place on wall

Purpose:

Prepare a forum for discussion on different issues and different positions on those issues

Directions:

1. On 5x7 cards place one topic on a card at a time. Place voting cards around the room. An example of voting cards: 5—strongly agree, 4—agree, 3—no opinion, 2—disagree, 1—strongly disagree. Each card has one number on it and the cards are placed around the room in sequence.

2. The topics should be relevant to the age of the participants and should have some controversy to insure different positions.

3. Once the topic has been announced, participants move to the area of the room which represents the position they hold.

4. At this time the leader can hold a discussion among the different groups (simultaneously) and then invite a speaker from each group to support the position of this group.

5. Members can then be given an opportunity to change positions if they have been convinced that another place would better represent their opinions.

6. Different topics are introduced and the process repeated until the leader discontinues.

Elizabeth S. Foster-Harrison

Suggested Topics:

- Capital Punishment
- Corporal Punishment in Schools
- Free child care for students who are parents
- Reduce drinking age to 15
- Increase driving speed to 65 on all four-lane roads
- Decrease age to obtain drivers license
- Allow off campus lunches for high schools
- College scholarships for need only
- Smoking in all schools for all personnel should be prohibited
- Males are better drivers
- Females are generally more caring than males

Processing:

a. Ask the members to reflect upon what they have learned about the other participants opinions.

b. Discuss how people can have different opinions and still get along. Can people discuss those differences without feeling anger or hostility?

c. What causes people to have no opinion?

d. Why is it so difficult to discuss areas of wide opinions?

Alternative:

Have the participants brainstorm a list of topics that they feel are particularly of interest to them.

Icebreaker 2.27
Labeling the Group

Time:

15 minutes

Materials:

Chart paper, cards, pen or pencil

Number of people:

10 to 40

Purpose:

To provide the group with information about each other without specifically asking direct questions to each member

Directions:

1. Give people four sticky labels on which they write their names.
2. They are to place their names (sticky labels) on four different charts.
3. The charts have a card above which is turned over so no one can see the topic.
4. Once all the names are stuck on the sheets, the topic cards are turned over and each person goes to the sheet and writes the information requested.
5. The sheets are then shared with the groups.

Topics:

1. List your three favorite ways to spend summer.
2. What wish would you make for a single day?
3. What makes you the happiest?
4. If you could give a family member a gift, what would it be and why?
5. What makes you angry?
6. What things do you like to read?

Alternative:

The topics could be written in a journal or essay and shared with others.

Processing:

Discuss what the group knows about its members.

Icebreaker 2.28
Capturing Your Group's Average

Number of People:

Unlimited

Time:

30 to 60 minutes

Materials:

Yard stick, measuring tapes, string

Purpose:

To provide an active way to gather information about the characteristics of a group. Group averages are calculated.

Directions:

1. Divide the participants into groups.

2. Identify specific information that each group must collect. They can report their findings on a chart or transparency.

3. The group's should be numbered, lettered or named and move as a group.

4. Areas to assign:

   - Average shoe size
   - Average Height
   - Average hand width
   - Average Arm spread from left fingertips to right
   - Average vertical jump
   - Average hair color
   - Average eye color
   - Average big toe length

5. Groups then return to summarize their findings and prepare a way to share the information with the entire group.

6. Each group presents its findings to the entire population, thus presenting a picture of the whole group.

Discussion:

a. What are common characteristics?

b. What would the "typical" person from this group look like?

Icebreaker 2.29
Meeting the New Person

Number of People:

Minimum 12

Time:

15 to 20 minutes

Materials:

Hand out for Who You Are?, flip chart paper, markers

Purpose:

To establish a sensitivity for what it feels like to be "new" and look at how different people might view the role.

Directions:

1. Explain to the participants that they are to assume that they are the New Kid on the Block. You could imagine other such "new" roles, such as the new teacher for the semester, or the new person on the job, or the new person in the neighborhood.

2. Hand out the sheet: "Who Are You?" Ask the participants to assume the different people on the sheet.

3. Group the members together by what role they selected. (An option is to assign the roles.)

4. The groups are to write questions that they might ask the "new person" from their specific perspective. You decide what they might want to know and why. Be sure to discuss this during the processing of the activity.

5. Have the groups place their questions and motives on flip chart paper and then post it.

Processing:

A. Discuss how it feels to be the new person and try to make good decisions about fitting in.

B. Answer: Why would the different people have different perspectives? Other roles: Principal, counselor, shy person, athlete, band member, artist.

Adaptation:

Use whatever roles are appropriate for the job function for the group participants.

Who Are You?

Teacher	New Person	Regular Student in Class	Gang Member

Elizabeth S. Foster-Harrison

Icebreaker 2.30
Opposites

Number of People:

Unlimited

Materials:

Copy of the Artwork on opposites

Time:

10 to 20 minutes

Purpose:

To look at different sides of personalities and varying attitudes

Directions:

1. Use the artwork on page 102 that shows a contrasting view of two objects that are the same, but different in light and dark contrast. This exercise is designed for people to analyze how people can look at a situation from two different perspectives. The key is the positive or negative attitude of the person involved that can make such a difference.

2. Either pass out the entire sheet or select opposite pictures to hand out to individual participants.

3. Ask the participants to discuss what the picture might represent in terms of characteristics related to the symbol.

4. Create different scenarios and ask people to write a response according to the picture that they have. Example: If a response if requested, then written—pair the two people who have the light sun, and the dark sun together to compare answers. Have the two with the dark moon and the light moon compare their responses.

Processing:

Have the group members discuss how certain attitudes or types of personalities can cloud a perspective. How can difficult situations be better with a positive attitude.

Scenario suggestions:

1. On the way to school Sue tripped and sprained her leg.

2. The weather was bad and Henry was unable to go to work.

3. Jill and Mary Ann had decided to go shopping, but Jill got sick.

4. George was disappointed when he got a "D" in history.

5. Carlin was really embarrassed when she came out of the grocery store and all her groceries fell out of the bag.

6. The storage shed that held all of the Smith's winter clothes was accidentally burned during the fall, when leaves being burned blew into the shed area and caught it on fire.

Create your own scenarios. They can be more elaborate if you like to see how people react to black and white situations.

Chapter III
Energizers

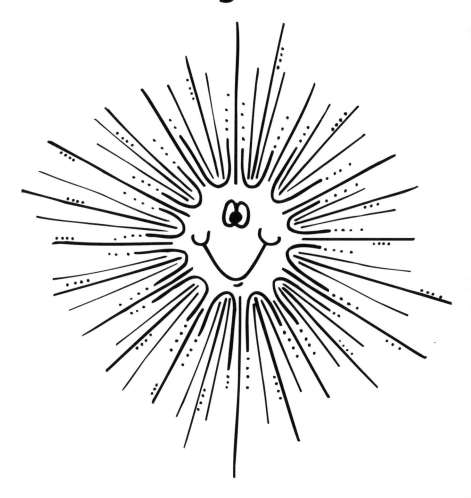

Elizabeth S. Foster-Harrison

Overview of Energizers

D.H. Conley faculty energized through dancing.

"What are energizers?" "What are the purposes behind energizers?" "Should everyone try energizers?" If you have asked those questions, you will want to read on for the answers.

Energizers are activities designed to actively stimulate and motivate the participants in your group, classroom, staff, or peer group. The uses are endless and yes, everyone who instructs or leads should use energizers during their sessions. The advantage of this approach is that it is both participatory and experiential. These activities are generally short, but they can be extended to last for longer periods. The participants feel involved and become committed to the tasks of the group. They will perform better and remain intellectually stimulated if their bodies and minds work together through involvement.

When should they be used? Energizers can be used at the beginning of a group session or class, or they can be used in the middle or at the end. When used at the beginning, the focus is usually to stimulate interest and focus the group. When used in the middle, it is often to keep the participants involved as they may tire during a long class or experience. At the end they can be used to reinstill or reinvigorate enthusiasm. Energizers can build skills and can be used as culminating activities.

Energizers are wonderful ways to involve people outside the typical chair and desk situation. Certain guidelines for success should be considered by the leader of the activity. Having fun does not mean lack of control, discipline, or management. In fact, successful energizers require a thorough understanding of the group's guidelines to assure that all participants continue to respect the rights of others and do not lose focus of the overall purpose of the activity.

You may want to refer to the beginning section on management to review the types of methods that will enhance the management and organization for using energizers. A few reminders as you begin:

1. Be thoroughly familiar with the activity and the materials necessary to carry out the activity.

2. Be consistent in providing the directions for the energizers and be sure that everyone listens to the directions. You may wish to model an example before the group begins. Give all the directions before the groups begin to move or have the groups get into their areas for work and then give the directions. Never try to talk over the group or talk while they are moving from one spot to another.

3. Be sure that everyone is familiar with the guidelines for functioning. It is always advantageous to have the participants assist in establishing the guidelines so that they have an investment in fulfilling the expectations.

4. Be prepared for a certain level of noise when involvement occurs. If you are timid about this, practice with smaller numbers to become acclimated to this type of activity. Remember that when people are relaxed and enjoying their tasks, they will be more likely to talk. As long as the noise and talk are productive, it is fine.

Elizabeth S. Foster-Harrison

5. Remember that the age of the participants in the group will determine the type of activity, the type of directions, and the length of processing. If working with young students, it is best to repeat directions twice, then give specific examples, and have group members repeat back or model what is expected. As the participants age—middle school, high, or adults—the directions will change as will the outcomes. Don't hesitate to let a group practice any of the activities or directions first before they begin if that will make them feel more comfortable.

6. Remember: You are the key to everything that happens in the activity. You must feel comfortable, demonstrate enthusiasm, participate, assist in processing, direct the progress and growth of the group, and provide the environment which supports this type of activity. Providing a structure—a type of framework—is necessary, but putting too many demands or limitations on the participants will inhibit the success of many of the activities. Use your good judgment in this area.

Growth is a personal phenomenon. It can happen before our eyes and it is fascinating to watch. Engaging students and other participants in activities which promote people interaction will enhance their growth and in turn all of those participating in both energizers and icebreakers!

Elizabeth S. Foster-Harrison

Energizer 3. 1
Shoop Shoop Song

Number of People:

Unlimited

Materials:

Copy of the Shoop Shoop Song Sheet

Time:

10 minutes

Skill:

Following directions

Directions:

Have the participants read (or sing along) with the Shoop Shoop Song. Divide the group in half and have the two groups stand in two lines facing each other. Each separate group should stand should to shoulder. Movements or gestures should be assigned to each group as appropriate from the song sheet. Once everyone has read through the song once, then the groups stand, sing, and carry out the movements. It feels like being with the Supremes in 1964!

Shoop Shoop Song Sheet
Is It In His Kiss

Does he love me? I want to know
How can I tell if he loves me so?
(cover heart)

Oh no you'll be deceived

Oh no he'll make believe
If you want to know, if he loves you so
It's in his kiss (point to lips)

Oh no it's just his charm

Oh no that's just his arm (point to arm)
If you want to know, if he loves you so
It's in his kiss (point to lips)

OOOH OOH it's in his kiss (point to lips)

Whoa-ooh Hug him and squeeze
    him tight (squeeze arms)
Find out what you want to know
If it's love, if it really is
It's there in his kiss (point to lips)

Oh no that's not the way
You're not listening to all I say
    (point to ears)
If you want to know, if he loves you so
It's in his kiss (point to lips)

Is it in his eyes?
(point to eyes)

Is it in his eyes?
(point to eyes)

That's where it is Oh Yeah!

Or is it in his face?
(point to face)

It's his warm embrace
(wrap arms)

That's where it is!
(point to lips)

That's where it is!
(point to lips)

How 'bout the way he acts?
(jump forward)

That's where it is!
(point to other members)

Elizabeth S. Foster-Harrison

Ooh It's in his kiss *(point to lips)*

That's where it is!
(point to other members)

Whoa-ooh Hug him and
   squeeze him tight *(squeeze)*
Find out what you want to know
If it's love, if it really is
It's there in his kiss *(point to lips)*

How 'bout the way he acts?
(jump forward)

Oh no that's not the way
You're not listening to all I say
   (point to ears)
If you want to know, if he loves you so
It's in his kiss *(point to lips)*

That's where it is!
(point finger at other group)

OOOH It's in his kiss *(point to lips)*

That's where it is!
(point finger at other group)

Ahh Yeah, It's in his kiss *(point to lips)*

That's where it is!
(point finger at other group)

Ooh It's in his kiss *(point to lips)*

That's where it is!
(point finger at other group)

It's in his kiss *(point to lips)*

That's where it is!
(point finger at other group)

It's in his kiss *(point to lips)*

That's where it is!
(point finger at other group)

Elizabeth S. Foster-Harrison

Energizer 3.2
Moving Paper Clips

Number of People:

Unlimited

Materials:

Paper clips and string

Time:

5 to 7 minutes

Skill:

Concentration (You might use this activity to introduce goal setting.)

Directions:

Have the participants tie a thin piece of string (approximately 10 inches long) to the top of a small paper clip. (An alternative to this would be to have all the clips ready with the string attached.) Have the participants hold the string in front of them with the string end in the fingers about eye height. The paper clip should be dangling at the end. Tell the participants to keep their hands still and just concentrate on the paper clip and think about moving the clip to the right and the left. Within about 30 seconds, everyone's paper clip should be swinging, just by concentrating on the clip, looking at it intensely, and thinking "moving" thoughts.

Note:

Introduce the participants to goal setting by discussing the importance of their vision and their determination. They can make things happen and change if they have enough direction and concentration. Then let them move the clips and wait for responses of surprise!

Thanks to Judy White for sharing this activity.

Energizer 3.3
Point North

Number of People:

Unlimited

Materials:

None

Time:

2 minutes

Directions:

Ask all participants to close their eyes for about 10 seconds and then ask them to remain with their eyes closed and to take their right hand and their pointer finger and point north. As soon as everyone is pointing, ask the participants to open their eyes. The group will be amused that fingers are pointing in all directions.

Discussion:

This activity is a good introduction to giving good directions or to understanding someone else's direction and interest. The point of this is to be sure that people examine their understanding of the direction in which they might be heading as well as other people and not to assume that everyone is headed the same way if it hasn't been discussed. (Direction is used in the context of decisions as well as a place of movement.)

Elizabeth S. Foster-Harrison

Energizer 3.4
Paint Brush

Number of People:

Unlimited

Materials:

None

Time:

5 minutes

Purpose:

To create fun and stimulate humor

Directions:

The group stands in front of the leader. The leader instructs the group to take their right hands and write their first names in the air. Next, they are asked to write their last names in the air with their left hands. (Usually that's more difficult.) Then tell the group that they have a chance to be more creative. Now they'll get to paint their first and last names; But, they have to put their hands behind their backs and pretend they have a paint brush embedded in their belly buttons and paint their names. Remember to dot every "i" and cross every "t." Enjoy the movement and laughter.

Alternatives to belly button:

Place paint brush in ear, in elbow, in hip, in mouth, in toe, in nose, on top of head, in the middle of the back.

Energizer 3.5
Now is the Time to Get Carded

Number of people:

Unlimited

Time:

A few minutes

Materials:

Copy of the "Card" Sheet

Purpose:

To provide a reflection opportunity for participants. Affirmations on these areas can be reinforcing

Directions:

Look at the next sheet. Duplicate that sheet to give to participants as appropriate for their use. If you prefer to copy only certain cards and reproduce them for use, then distribute them individually at the best time .

Processing:

Discuss how having the traits on each of the cards can be helpful in times of stress, irritation, or disappointment. Discuss how group members can better support each other through the actual implementation of the traits on the cards. Answer: How could a person in a helping situation be a better helper by integrating these cards and traits into their helping behavior?

Elizabeth S. Foster-Harrison

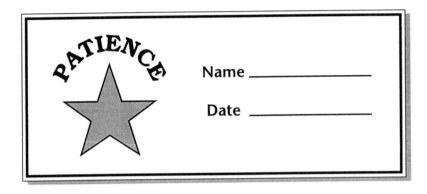

PATIENCE

Name _____

Date _____

I CARE

Name _____

Date _____

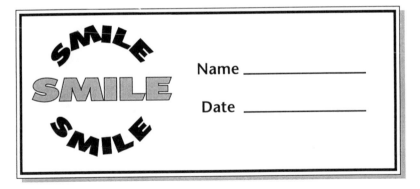

SMILE SMILE SMILE

Name _____

Date _____

Energizer 3.6
Grammar Review

Number of people:

Unlimited

Time

10 minutes

Materials:

Copy of The Story

Purpose:

To identify parts of speech and focus on listening skills

Focus of this energizer:

Pronouns

Note:

This energizer can be used with any subject matter and can be adapted to the special content and skill by rewriting the story.

Directions:

1. The participants are assigned something to do when they hear a certain part of speech.
2. When the participants hear a subject pronoun, they are to stomp their feet.
3. When they hear a possessive pronoun, they clap their hands.
4. When they hear an object pronoun, they stand up.

Modification:

The participants can raise their arms over their heads, wave them around if the foot stomping is a problem.

Note:

The directions should be posted, as well as read.

The Story:

"I am late," cried Mrs. Brown. She slammed her finger in her desk drawer while hurrying out of her office.

"Don't get another speeding ticket," warned Mr. Buchanan. She gave him a dirty look.

In the parking lot, she raced her engine, checked her gas level and threw the car in gear. It reversed right into the superintendent's new Ferrari. He sat behind his steering wheel crying. "You have ruined my new car!" he yelled.

"I am so sorry, Mr. Boss! I feel just terrible about this, but I'm in a hurry. Will you move this wreck out of my way?" asked Mrs. Brown.

"Where on earth are you going? Your mission better be important."

"My court date for a speeding ticket is today. I am due in traffic court. Mine is a lost cause now. I'm late and I can't defend myself."

"What defense have you? Get into the office and call a wrecker for me!"

"Mr. Buchanan, what wrecker service do you suggest I call?" asked Mrs. Brown, as she glumly sat in her desk chair by the phone.

"Call Acme Movers and Shakers and while you are at it, call for some driving lessons. The need for instruction today is yours!"

Thanks to Bonnie Kane of Rocky Mount, NC for this activity. Bonnie is a middle school teacher and an avid user and designer of energizers.

Energizer 3.7
Boat Ride

Number of People:

Unlimited

Materials:

Boat Ride Story

Time:

5 to 7 minutes

Skills:

Listening, following directions

Directions:

Place the movements that are associated with the words (listed below) on newsprint or a board so the participants can easily see them. Review the movements at least once prior to reading the storm report. Once the group is familiar with the movements and terms, read the report and the entire group should follow along, acting out the movements as they learn the words read in the story.

sunny = hands around smiling face

flying fish = fly in air with your arms

boat = jumping porpoises = jump up

waves = whole group wave

whale = two people join together and swim

breezes = whistle

eye to eye = make circle with fingers around eyes

fish = mouth shaped like fish

Elizabeth S. Foster-Harrison

Boat Ride Story

It was a sunny day when we went for our boat ride. The waves were low at the beginning of the morning so the boat didn't rock much. The breezes were cool and we started catching fish. As our sunny day progressed, the waves got higher... and higher, but the fish kept coming. We saw flying fish and jumping porpoises. The flying fish moved carelessly through the cool breezes. Soon the waves got higher than the side of the boat and we saw a huge whale. The whale looked eye to eye at us and we changed direction. The flying fish followed, the jumping porpoises followed, the breezes blew hard, and our sunny day took the boat to the dock in a hurry!

Energizer 3.8
Weather Storm Report

Number of People:

Unlimited

Materials:

Storm Report

Time:

5 to 7 minutes

Skills:

Listening, following directions

Directions:

Place the movements that are associated with the words (listed below) on newsprint or a board so the participants can easily see them. Review the movements at least once prior to reading the storm report. Once the group is familiar with the movements and terms, read the report and the entire group should follow along, acting out the movements as they learn the words read in the story.

rain = light tapping on table

lightning = body form thunderbolt

colder, colder, colder = brrrrrr

snow = fingers high in air dropping snow

wind = whistle

hail = paper balls or styrofoam

thunder = shake paper

storm = all sounds

high wind = shhhhhhh

Storm Report Story

As we watched our television, we could hear the rain softly tapping on the roof. It didn't take long to know a change was coming. It was getting colder and colder and colder. The weather pattern showed high wind, thunder, and lightning. The rain seemed to get louder and we heard our first crash of thunder. Though it was unusual, there was thunder with snow! Lots of pretty snow flakes! Soon, however, the snow flakes changed amidst the wind which was a high wind with thunder. We saw large hail heading our way and, in fact, we heard the hail on the roof. Next was a bolt of lightning—so unusual for a winter storm, but there it was. It was still getting colder and colder. But since we were in our heated and warm house, the storm didn't affect us!

Energizer 3.9
What's the Relay Today?

Number of People:

Unlimited, but keep teams of six as the maximum number per row/per group.

Materials:

Listed by each relay (A timer is needed for all relays.)

Time:

10 to 15 minutes for each relay

Purpose:

To provide a variety of ways to create a cooperative spirit and build group cohesion

Directions:

In each relay the people in the groups line up facing the person's back standing in front of them. There should be a leader in the front of the vertical row. The goal for the groups is to beat the total time it takes for the whole group to finish. There has to be a qualifying round and then the "real" round. If you want to be competitive, instruct the individual groups to set individual times and then the whole group tries to beat the best score of the individual group.

Fly Swatter Balloon Relay:

(You need a dozen plastic fly swatters and balloons.) This can be done with one person per group or pairs from each group that move together. The pairs will need a bit more space. The object is to keep a balloon afloat in the air from the beginning point to the destination and return without it falling to the floor. If the balloon falls, the participant must return to the front of the line and begin again. If pairs go from each group, the balloon is hit between the two and alternating. One person hits and then the second and then the first and so on. (Hint: sometimes going faster puts you farther behind. The air resistance increases with more movement.)

Peacock Feather Relay:

(You need about a dozen peacock feathers.) These can be obtained from a peacock farm.... but if that's not an easy task, try a variety store like Pier One Imports.

The peacock feather is placed in the palm of the hand—the quill side on the palm. The participants are not to let the feather drop, not to touch it with the other hand nor hold it between the fingers. The quill should sit in the middle of a flat palm. If the feather falls, the person returns to the line and begins again. Tell the participants (after they've done it once) that if they concentrate on looking at the eye of the feather, the balance will be improved 100%.

Bubble Blow Relay:

(You need six small bottles of soap bubble.) The participants line up and are instructed to pair with a partner in their group. The pair from each group runs the race with one person holding the bubble bottle and bubble blower, while the partner blows bubbles through the whole race.

Energizer 3.10
Whose Penny or Potato?

Number of People:

20 people, or smaller groups of 8 each

Materials:

Potatoes or pennies

Time:

20 minutes

Purpose:

To increase observation skills

Skills:

Increase ability to focus on detail and characteristics

Directions:

Place group members in a sitting circle. Have a potato for each member. Instruct members to spend one minute memorizing every detail about their potato. After one minute put all the potatoes in a bag—shake up and place on the floor in the center of the circle. Members are to find their own potato and describe to others how they knew which was theirs. Members must not indent, scratch, or mark their potato in any way.

Discussion:

How can noticing detail be helpful on working with others or working in a group?

Alternatives:

1. Use pennies of the same years. All must be the same year or no more that 2 or 3 different years, so the focus is on other characteristics rather that the year. Other coins could be used.

2. Socks of the same color.

3. Used pencils

4. Carrots or Apples could be used. After being washed, they could be eaten.

Elizabeth S. Foster-Harrison

Energizer 3.11
Rhythm Sticks

Number of People:

Unlimited

Materials:

Record, Music, Sticks

Time:

10 minutes per selection

Purposes:

To provide practice in working as a group

Creating a group rhythm reinforced through sound

Directions:

1. Leaders can use for the sticks, 1/4" dowel rods and have them cut in 10" to 12" lengths.

2. Use any number of rhythm records, either commercial records or contemporary music for the groups to use to beat out the rhythm. This is fun and creates camaraderie.

3. Suggestions for Rhythm Stick Commercial Tapes—

    a. Rhythm Stick Activities (Tape) (Ages 5-9, but can be used for older groups) 4EA55 $10.95

    b. Lively Music for Rhythm Stick Fun (Tape) (Ages 8-12, but can be used for older groups) 4KB2000 $10.95

    These can be ordered from:

    Educational Record Center

    3233 Burnt Mill Dr., Suite 100

    Wilmington, NC 28403-2655

    1-800-438-1637

Energizer 3.12
Mummy Wrap

Number of people:

15 to 25

Materials:

Toilet tissue roll (1 per team of 3 to 4)

1 roll masking tape

Time:

15 to 20 minutes

Purpose:

To develop group cohesion and group trust

Directions:

Every team of 3 to 4 receives a roll of toilet tissue. One member of the group is designated as the mummy. The other team members are given 5 minutes to wrap their mummy with the roll of tissue paper. The masking tape is used to keep the paper from separating or tearing. The mummy should be wrapped from head to toe, but with some leg movement so walking is possible. At the end of 5 minutes, wrapping stops and the team members walk their mummy around the room. Care must be taken to be sure the mummy doesn't get hurt or bumped. Team members should gently move their mummies. A race could be held with teams racing their mummies.

Discussion:

1. How does it feel to be confined and have to rely on others?

2. What times created some anxiety?

3. How careful were the group members?

4. How can we depend on others as well as use our skills as helpers or guides?

Elizabeth S. Foster-Harrison

Energizer 3.13
Dot to Dot and Other Variations

Number of People:

Unlimited

Materials:

Colored sticky dots, or sticky numbers, or labels

Time: 10 to 15 minutes

Purpose:

Can be used to teach discrimination between colors or numbers for the younger participants

Directions:

This is a variation of "Ghost to Ghost" from *Energizers and Icebreakers, Book 1,* Energizer 2.10, p. 82.

1. You need an odd number of people for this activity.

2. Have everyone pair up and the odd person stands in the center of the group as the caller.

3. If working with young children, place 4 different colored sticky dots on each child. Each child will have 4 different colors, but all members will have same 4 colors—such as red, green, blue, and yellow.

4. Instruct the caller to call out particular colors. Each pair matches their colors to their partners. Such as: red to red means wherever one person's red dot is, it is touched to the other person's red dot.

5. On the third or fourth color called, the caller yells "dot to dot" and everyone changes partners.

6. People may not have the same partner. The caller tries to get a partner, so everyone needs to scramble to get a partner.

7. The person without a partner is the next caller.

Variations:

Use numbers to match	(Number to Number)
Use fruits to match	(Fruit to Fruit)
Use vegetables to match	(Vegetable to Vegetable)
Use hats that represent jobs	(Hat to Hat)
Use animals to match	(Animal to Animal)
Use answers to math problems	(Math to Math)
Use synonyms or antonyms to match	(Synonym to Synonym)
	(Antonym to Antonym)

Energizer 3.14
Body Crostics

Number of People:

Unlimited

Materials:

Blackboard or poster board

Time:

10 minutes

Purpose:

To develop group cohesion

Directions:

1. The person with the longest name places it on the blackboard or large poster board.

2. Like name crostics, participants all connect their first name to the person with the longest first name, who has written that name on the board.

3. Once everyone has written their name, the group actually connects their hands so their bodies assume the same position as the name crostic on the board. Last names are then added to the board and people must again attach so that some part of their body is in touch with the location of their first & last name.

Refer to Icebreaker 1.24, "Name Crostics" in *Energizers and Icebreakers, Book 1* for more information on utilizing name crostics.

Energizer 3.15
Patty Cake Games

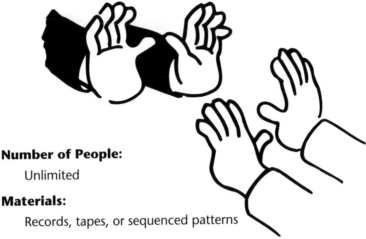

Number of People:

Unlimited

Materials:

Records, tapes, or sequenced patterns

Time:

5 to 15 minutes

Purpose:

This energizer can help develop focus and attention

Skills:

Rhythm, detail, and listening skills, hand-eye coordination

Directions:

Members are placed in pairs and asked to face each other. Prearranged routines can be designed for partners to use. The "old" patty cake games of the past still work—just consider some new, more complex sequences.

Certain commercial materials are available with patterns for the patty cake and they can be used to develop hand-eye coordination, or listening skills.

1. Clap, Snap, & Tap (Tape by Ambrose Brazelton) 4EA48 $10.95

2. Body Jive (Tape) 4EA96 $10.95

These can be ordered from:

Educational Record Center
3233 Burnt Mill Dr., Suite 100
Wilmington, NC 28403-2655
1-800-438-1637

Energizer 3.16
Thread Groups

Number of People:

Unlimited

Materials:

One full spool of thread per group

Time:

10 to 15 minutes

Purpose:

To provide group cohesion and a way to really feel connected

Directions:

1. Have the participants organized together in groups of 6 or 8 and form lines with each group member elbow to elbow, one group in front of the other.

2. Give a spool of thread to the first person in each line instructing each to tie the thread to the end of a finger.

3. The spool should be passed to each group member by first passing the spool of thread through the clothing of each member from down the neck, through the waist, and out the bottom of the pants or skirt.

4. Once the group gets the thread to the end of the line, form a circle and, while they all are still connected, toss a balloon to each group.

Elizabeth S. Foster-Harrison

5. The groups should keep the balloon in the air with different body parts as the leader calls them out. All members should hold hands. Keep the balloon up with:

   a. your hands

   b. your wrists

   c. your knees

   d. your elbows

   e. your shoulders

   f. your thighs

   g. your toes

   h. your head

   The leader can vary the parts and instruct the groups to move wherever necessary to keep the balloon in the air.

6. The thread can be pulled out through all the members.

Processing:

Talk about how it felt to be connected as a group and how much better that felt than pulling apart.

Energizer 3. 17

Follow the Commands: Before and Before

Number of People:

Unlimited

Materials:

None necessary

Time:

10 minutes

Purpose:

Listening and concentrating

Directions:

1. One person serves as the leader and stands facing the group of people who are also standing.

2. At the first level, the group follows the leader like in Simon Says: "Touch you head" & the group touches their heads. "Touch your toes," and so forth. There is no need to wait for "Simon."

3. After about 5 directions, tell the group that they really need to concentrate. Listen to the directions, but only follow the one given one time previously. Example: Touch your head—Group does nothing

    Touch your toes—Group touches head

    Touch your waist—Group touches toes

    Touch your lip—Group touches waist and so forth.

4. Give the group time to practice. Once they have mastered one time back—go to two behind. Example:

    Touch your head—Group does nothing

    Touch your toes—Group does nothing

    Touch your waist—Group touches head

    Touch your lips—Group touches toes etc.

   This is more difficult. Tell group members that if they get lost, they should just stop & listen & they'll catch up.

Elizabeth S. Foster-Harrison

5. Once this is mastered, pair the members and start over having each touch the part on their partner. This just adds an interesting variation.

Source for ideas listed below:

a. Clap, Snap, & Tap (Tape by Ambrose Brazelton) 4EA48 $10.95

b. Body Jive (Tape) 4EA96 $10.95

These can be ordered from:

Educational Record Center
3233 Burnt Mill Dr., Suite 100
Wilmington, NC 28403-2655

1-800-438-1637

Elizabeth S. Foster-Harrison

Energizer 3.18
Banding Your Groups: Tag 1

Number of People:

Unlimited

Materials:

An elastic band—2 yards in length, sewn to form a circle & 2" wide

Time:

10 minutes

Purpose:

Provide movement, team spirit

Directions:

The activity is a variation on the "Triangle Tag" activity, described in *Energizers and Icebreakers, Book 1*, p. 140.

1. Members form teams of 4.

2. Three of the four place the rubber band on the outside of their waists and form a triangle. The participants are told to put their hands behind their back and to maintain the triangle shape with the band.

3. One member of the triangle is "it" while the outside member of the group must tag it. The outside member may not reach across the group and must tag "it" by actually running around to "it."

4. Once "it" is tagged, the outside person is "it" and they change places.

Discussion:

The next 5 "banding" energizers allow groups to work together for a common purpose. Ask groups to focus on their tasks and describe why they were successful in each case. What must each group do to be successful?

Energizer 3.19
Geometric Bands

Number of People:

Unlimited

Materials:

An elastic band—2 yards in length, sewn to form a circle & 2" wide

Time:

15 minutes

Purpose:

To review different mathematical geometric shapes

Directions:

1. The groups are given 5 to 7 minutes to plan how they will demonstrate different geometric shapes. They must use the bands and their bodies to demonstrate the shapes.

2. Each group goes one at a time, demonstrating one shape; then another group proceeds. No one group repeats another's shape. This continues until there are no more shapes.

3. As each shape is shown, the other groups are asked to name the shape.

Elizabeth S. Foster-Harrison

Energizer 3.20
Band Up—Band Down

Number of People:

Unlimited

Materials:

An elastic band—2 yards in length, sewn to form a circle & 2" wide

Time:

6 minutes

Purpose:

To develop group cohesion and identity

Directions:

1. The members are asked to stand in a circle of 6 to 8 members.

2. The elastic band is put on the outside of the circle around the waists of the members.

3. The members are instructed to put their arms around the waists of the people on each side of them.

4. The band is then supposed to be moved to the ankles of the group—up to the shoulders and back to the waist. No hands can be used & the band cannot drop to the floor. If it does, the group starts over at the waist.

5. By wiggling up, down, left, right, and around, the group can control where the band moves. Lots of giggles and laughs accompany this one.

Energizer 3 .21
Rubber Bands Around

Number of People:

Unlimited

Materials:

An elastic band—2 yards in length, sewn to form a circle & 2" wide

Time:

5 to 7 minutes

Purpose:

To encourage group development and support

Directions:

1. The participants are directed to group together in 6 to 8 member groups.

2. Everyone in each group is asked to hold hands. The leader takes one band to each group and hangs the band over the wrist of one person in each group. Hands need to be held after the band is placed.

3. The groups are instructed to pass the band around the group - over the heads and under the feet until it has passed through the entire group.

4. There are a variety of ways to accomplish this task. Groups like to compete to see who can move the band all the way around the quickest. Use a timer—give groups several opportunities to decrease their time and have each group demonstrate their quickest or most creative method.

Energizer 3.22
Music Bands

Number of People:

Unlimited

Materials:

Tapes of different kinds of music, An elastic band—2 yards in length, sewn to form a circle 2" wide

Time:

10 minutes

Purpose:

To create an entertaining way to develop group consensus and fun

Directions:

1. Place the members in groups of 4.

2. Instruct the groups to place the rubber band around the outside of the waists of the group.

3. The groups are given 5 minutes to plan different movements they could make—feet, hands, body, when the music comes on. They should move to the rhythm—the beat—and if the music changes, so should the rhythm, timing, and speed.

Note:

Leaders select pieces with a prominent beat. Music choices such as: "Can't Touch This" (Hammer); "Pink Cadillac," "I'm So Excited," or "Jump" (Pointer Sisters); "Electric Slide." Vary the music by adding some classical, some country and some waltzes. It's a good, relaxation opener for groups that have been together for awhile.

Elizabeth S. Foster-Harrison

Energizer 3.23
Do You Match Now?

Number of People:

10 to 20

Time:

5 to 10 minutes

Materials:

A bell and a trading card for all participants

Purpose:

Exchanging items to identify another person's feelings based on wearing or sharing items

Directions:

1. Instruct the participants to stand in a circle. Then ask them to turn to their right to find a partner. Use the Trading Card sheet on page 146.

2. Tell them that when they hear the bell, they should exchange something with their partner. They should record the person's name and the item they trade.

3. This continues 3, 4, 5 times until the participants have nothing more of their own to trade. The participants should not give away someone else's item, only their own. They continue to change partners every time the bell rings.

4. Individuals in the group then share what it feels like to be an amalgamation of other people. The items traded could be clothing, items in a purse or wallet, jewelry, watches, and so forth. They should put on, wear, or hold the items as they should be used.

Processing:

1. The sharing of feelings involves identifying feelings that are comfortable and those that aren't.

2. What items more likely represent someone else than you. Why?

Do You Match Now? Trading Card

You traded what?	To whom?	How does it feel?

Elizabeth S. Foster-Harrison

Energizer 3.24
The Pop-Up Paulsons

Number of People:

18

Materials:

Copy of the story

Time:

10 minutes

Directions:

1. Listed below are the main characters in the story.

1. Paula	6. Pamela	11. Professor
2. Peter	7. Grand Pappy	12. Poplar Trees(2)
3. Papa	8. Grand Mammy	13. Pennies (2)
4. Pepe	9. Petla	14. Popsicles (2)
5. Pig	10. Petunias(2)	

2. When the story is read, the specific characters whose name are read, jump up, touch their toes and say "Uh, huh!" The Pig should also OINK. The Popsicles should lick their "pretend" popsicles. The Petunia's pretend to grow and spread their petals from the ground up and the Professor stands up with a pointer to start to give a lecture. The Poplar trees should wave in the wind. Whenever the "Paulsons" are named as a family, everyone jumps up and responds.

Adaptation:

1. More than one person can assume the roles so that the number participating will enlarge.

2. You can have name plates for people so they know who they are and others do, too. Just tying string on a name sign allows the name to hang on the front on the character.

The Story

PAULA PAULSON and PETER PAULSON were brother and sister. PAPA PAULSON loved his children PAULA and PETER. He also loved PINKY, his PIG and all the PETUNIAS in the yard. PINKY, the PIG used to bother the mail carrier, PAMELA, who generally picked a PETUNIA on her daily route. PAMELA also talked daily to PAPA PAULSON along with GRAND PAPPY and GRAND MAMMY. The POPLAR TREES were shading the porch for GRAND PAPPY and GRAND MAMMY and in the summer, the POPLAR TREES kept it cool so GRAND PAPPY and GRAND MAMMY could eat their POPSICLES. PETULA, a friend of PAULA and PETER'S always came to play on Wednesday and brought her PENNIES so they could pitch PENNIES. On Wednesdays, the PROFESSOR came to visit PAPA to talk about PEPE, the new barber who wanted to buy PINKY, the PIG. GRAND PAPPY and GRAND MAMMY got upset under the POPLARS when the PROFESSOR suggested that PEPE buy PINKY the PIG. PAMELA delivered the mail, picked her PETUNIAS, and said that PAULA and PETER would be distressed with PINKY the PIG gone. The PAULSON family wasn't interested in selling PINKY the PIG to PEPE, so the PROFESSOR told the PAULSON family that PEPE could look elsewhere. GRAND PAPPY and GRAND MAMMY were happier now under the POPLARS licking their POPSICLES. PETULA smiled and pitched her PENNIES with PAULA and PETER. PAPA said good-bye to the PROFESSOR and the PAULSON family was satisfied.

Elizabeth S. Foster-Harrison

Energizer 3.25
Wrap Up—"In the Eye of the Beholder"

Number of People:

Unlimited

Time:

10 to 15 minutes

Materials:

Variety of objects or pictures

Purpose:

To provide reflection on what an object can mean to a group/ group experience

Directions:

1. Collect a variety of pictures, objects, words, and photos. Simple things can be used as well as more complicated. These objects can be placed in a box, a bag, on the wall or on a table. You can use pictures from page 150.

2. Ask the members to identify how the object has positive symbolism for the group, the group experience or training. It could tie directly to a concept, or concluding concepts for an entire curriculum.

Telephone	Boat	Cow	Clock	Dog
Sun	Pencil	Paintbrush	Book	Piece of Jewelry

Examples of some comments you might expect or try to develop from some of the above items could include:

Telephone—Important to stay in touch, networking, communication

Sun—A bright reminder of what our disposition could be like

Boat—We can venture out into new waters

Pencil—Collect your thoughts for reflection

Cow—An animal always giving something

Paintbrush—Something that gives color, art, design and beautifies the world

Book—A way of always learning—never too old to learn

Jewelry—Like the experience, something to cherish

Examples of pictures that you can use.

Elizabeth S. Foster-Harrison

Energizer 3.26
Put Downs or Put Ups?

Number of People:
Unlimited

Materials:
Bowl or bag to put slips of paper in

Purpose:
To sensitize the participants to the effect of put-downs, as well as to practice distinguishing between a put-down and a compliment

Directions:
1. Ask the members to make a list of different compliments they could give to someone.
2. Then have the members make a list of "put downs" they have heard in the past weeks.
3. These are then placed on strips of paper and put in a bowl or bag.
4. The slips are drawn out one at a time and read aloud.
5. The group decides whether the slip of paper reflects a compliment or a put down.
6. If it is a put-down, the group is to reword it so it can be a PUT-UP! This gives everyone practice in discriminating between the difference between a compliment and a put-down.

Discussion:
This should include an opportunity to talk about how it feels to be put down and what kinds of reactions are appropriate, as well as inappropriate when that happens. A board or flip chart can be kept with the kinds of PUT-UPS the group created.

Energizer 3.27
Toe Fencing

Number of People:

Unlimited, use three in a group

Amount of Time:

3 to 5 minutes

Materials:

Rolled newspaper "foils," taped with bright tape

Purpose:

To develop trust

Directions:

1. The members are paired and asked to put one hand on their forehead, while their other hand holds the foil.

2. In pairs of two, with flat shoes, or barefooted- the pair tries to hit each other's toes three times with the "foil." As each person attempts to hit the other person, the individual protects his/her own toes without letting the opponent touch them.

3. The third person is the judge and keeps track of who has been hit and who has not. The judge reminds participants to keep one hand on the forehead to protect eyes and can stop the action if the movement is too ferocious.

Processing:

This can be a fun activity with a lot of movement. Discuss the role of the judge and how competition instills motivation. Question: Can too much competition interfere with cooperation?

Thanks to Mary Lou Diener and Marilyn Routh of Asheboro City Schools, Asheboro, North Carolina who contributed this activity during a "Make and Take Workshop" for their system.

Energizer 3.28
This is Your Life: Hollywood!

Number of People:

20 to 25

Amount of Time:

45 minutes

Materials:

Markers and construction paper or poster board sheets

Purpose:

To create drama out of everyday life

Note:

This activity will involve storyboarding. Storyboarding is a method of telling a story or illustrating concepts through individual mats or sheets of paper. Each individual sheet would represent a drawn picture and the sheets would be illustrated in sequence. Imagine it as similar to the pictures you see when animated films are created. One picture per movement. In this case it is one picture per activity/event/celebration/concept. This idea can be used to illustrate many different ideas.

Directions:

1. Be sure to make everyone feel like they could be stars or playwrights, because everyone has a story to tell.

2. This can be done in pairs, trios, or singly, depending on the number of people involved.

3. A particular segment of one's life is determined that could be told through a series of storyboards. Because of the time, probably an entire lifetime would be too comprehensive. Select some special time, moment, celebration or series of important events. The boards are all illustrated.

4. Members work on their storyboards. On the back they identify their stories by name and the number of the sequence on each card.

5. By identifying the number on the back, cards can be exchanged making new stories.

6. This can be a very creative activity and one that allows great insight into events in people's lives.

Variation:

If a group makes a story, then each member can hold a card in front while the group tells the story.

Processing:

This can take time to give everyone sufficient "center stage" to move their storyboards and tell their story. Give everyone time. A modification of this would include sharing within a group.

Video Cross-Reference

Energizers and Icebreakers—The Video is available through Educational Media Corporation, Box 21311, Minneapolis, MN 55421, for $39.95. The activities that are shown on that video are listed below in the general sequence in which they occur on the video. This cross-referencing should be helpful so you can find the specific directions for any of the activities you see and would like to try. The activities can be found in *Energizers and Icebreakers for All Ages and Stages* (Book 1, 1989) or *More Energizers and Icebreakers for All Ages and Stages* (Book 2, 1994). Both books are available through Educational Media Corporation.

1. **Balloon Stomp**

   Book 1: Energizer 2.51, p. 156

   Title: The Backside Shuffle

2. **Bean Bag Toss**

   Book 2: Icebreaker 2.6, p. 55

   Title: Three New Friends

3. **Body Profile**

   Book 1: Icebreaker 1.34, p. 62

   Title: Body Profile

4. **All About You**

   Book 1: Icebreaker 1.5, p. 10

   Title: All About You

5. **Animal Friends**

   Book 1: Energizer, 2.32, p. 121

   Title: Animal Friends

6. **Wrapping your Mummy**

   Book 2: Energizer 3.12, p. 130

   Title: Mummy Wrap

7. **Boat Ride**

   Book 2: Energizer 3.7, p. 122

   Title: Boat Ride

8. **Thread Group**

   Book 2: Energizer 3.16, p. 134

   Title: Thread Groups

9. **Music Bands**

   Book 2: Energizer 3.22, p. 144

   Title: Music Bands

10. **Group Lap**

    Book 1: Energizer 2.11, p. 85

    Title: The Group Lap

11. **Who Has the Star?**

    Book 1: Energizer 2.34, p. 125

    Title: Applause

12. **The Scarf**

    Book 1: Energizer 2.29, p. 115

    Title: What's the Scarf?

13. **Feeling Bag**

    Book 2: Icebreaker 2.19, p. 80

    Title: The Feeling Bag

14. **Fly Swatter and Balloon Relay**

    Book 2: Energizer 3.9, p. 126

    Title: What's the Relay Today?

15. **Triangle Tag**

    Book 1: Energizer 2.42, p. 140

    Title: Tag Variations

    Book 2: Energizer 3.18, p. 139

    Title: Banding Your Groups: Tag 1

16. **Bands Around**

    Book 2: Energizer 3.21, p. 142

    Title: Rubber Bands Around

17. **Cracker Jack Box**

    Book 2: Icebreaker 2.20, p. 81

    Title: Crackerjacks

18. **Rabbit and Carrot**

    Book 1: Energizer 2.7, p. 77

    Title: The Rabbit and the Carrot

Elizabeth S. Foster-Harrison

19. Dot to Dot
Book 2: Energizer 3.13, p. 131
Title: Dot to Dot and Other Variations

20. Flower to Flower
Book 1: Energizer 2.10, p. 82
Title: Ghost to Ghost
Book 2: Energizer 3.13, p. 131
Title: Dot to Dot and Other Variations

21. Bubble Blow Relay
Book 2: Energizer 3.9, p. 126
Title: What's the Relay Today?

22. Paper Bag Relay
Book 2: Energizer 3.9, p. 126
Title: What's the Relay Today?

23. Peacock Feather Relay
Book 2: Energizer 3.9, p. 126
Title: What's the Relay Today?

24. Paper Plate
Book 1: Icebreaker 1.19, p. 35
Title: Make the Back the Sunny Side

25. Group Graphing
Book 2: Icebreaker 2.1, p. 33
Title: Group Profile

26. Help
Book 1: Energizer 2.18, p. 99
Title: Help

27. Cooperative Puzzle
Book 1: Energizer 2.13, p. 89
Title: Puzzling Puzzles

28. Three New Games
Book 2: Icebreaker 2.7, p. 58
Title: Three New Groups

Contacting the Author

If you are interested in workshops, clinics, staff development, or institutes on the utilization of energizers and icebreakers in your work area, please feel free to get in touch at the address below.

If you make modifications, alterations or additions to energizers and think they are important to other users, drop a note to the address below.

If you design your own energizers and icebreakers and would like to contribute to the next edition of a new energizers and icebreakers book, just send your name, address, phone number and activity description to the address below. Using the same format in this book would be helpful in structuring your activity.

Good luck in your endeavors!!!!

Dr. Elizabeth S. Foster-Harrison
Department of Elementary and Middle Grades Education
School of Education
East Carolina University
Greenville, NC 27858

919-757-6833 (work phone)

919-355-1092 (fax) Games and Energizers

Bibliography

Barry, S.A. (1987). *The world's best party games.* New York, NY: Sterling Publishing.

Bentley, M.B. (1976). *Indoor and outdoor games.* Belmont, CA: David S. Lake Publishers.

Chihak, M.K., and Heron, B.J. (1980). *Games children should play. Sequential lessons for teaching communication skills in grades K-6.* Santa Monica, CA: Goodyear Publishing.

Cottrell J. (1975). *Teaching with creative dramatics.* Skokie, IL: National Textbook.

Fleugelman, A. (ed.). (1978). *The new games book.* Tiburon, CA: Headlands Press.

Fleugelman, A. (ed.). (1981). *More new games!* Tiburon, CA: Headlands Press.

Forbess-Greene, S. (1983). *Encyclopedia of icebreakers.* San Diego, CA: University Associates, Inc.

Foster, E. (1989). *Energizers and icebreakers for all ages and stages.* Minneapolis, MN: Educational Media Corporation.

Hughes, R.S., & Kloeppel, P. (1994). *S.A.I.L.: Self-Awareness in language arts.* Minneapolis, MN: Educational Media Corporation.

Hazouri, S.P., & McLaughlin, M.S. (1993). *Warm ups & wind downs: 101 activities for moving and motivating groups.* Minneapolis, MN: Educational Media Corporation.

Kamu, C., & DeVries, R. (1980). *Group games in early childhood.* Washington, DC: The National Association for Education of Young Children.

LeFevre, D.N. (1988). *New games for the whole family.* New York, NY: Putnam Publishing Co.

Lehr, J.B., & Martin, C. (1992). *We're all at risk: Inviting learning for everyone.* Minneapolis, MN: Educational Media Corporation.

Luvmour, S., & Luvmour, J. (1990). *Everyone wins! Cooperative games & activities.* Philadelphia, PA: New Society Publishers.

Metzner, S. (1986). *One-minute game guide-chalkboard learning games for the elementary grades.* Belmont, CA: Fearon Pitman Publishers.

Michaelis, B, and Michaelis, D. (1977). *Learning through noncompetitive activities and play.* Palo Alto, CA: Learning Handbooks.

Mill, C. (1980). *Activities for trainers: 50 useful designs.* San Diego, CA: University Associates.

Pfiefer, J.W., and Jones, J.E. (1973). *A handbook of structured experiences for human relations training, Vol. IV.* San Diego, CA: University Associates.

Pfeifer, J.W., and Jones, J.E. (1980). *The 1980 handbook for group facilitators.* San Diego, CA: University Associates.

Renard, S., & Sockol, K. (1993). *The collaborative process: enhancing self-concepts through k-6 group activities.* Minneapolis, MN: Educational Media Corporation.

Rohnke, K. (1989). *Cowstails and cobras II: A guide to games, initiatives, ropes courses, & adventure curriculum.* Dubuque, Iowa: Kendall/Hunt Publishing.

Rohnke, K. (1984). *A guide to initiative problems, adventure games and trust activities.* Dubuque, Iowa: Kendall/Hunt Publishing.

Rowen, L. (1990). *Beyond winners: sports & games all kids want to play.* Carthage, Ill: Fearon Publications.

Weinstein, M., and Goodman, J. (1980). *Playfair.* San Luis Obispo, CA: Impact Publishers.

Wenc, C.C. (1993). *Cooperation: Learning through laughter,* (second edition). Minneapolis, MN: Educational Media Corporation.

Wrek, B. (1992). *Holiday games & activities.* Florissant, MO: Human Kinetics Books.

Yaconelli, M. and Rice W. (1979). *Super ideas for youth groups.* Grand Rapids, MI: Zondervan Publishing House.

Elizabeth S. Foster-Harrison